Fundamentals of
Technical Services

ALA FUNDAMENTALS SERIES

FUNDAMENTALS FOR THE ACADEMIC LIAISON
by Richard Moniz, Jo Henry, and Joe Eshleman

FUNDAMENTALS OF CHILDREN'S SERVICES, 2ND ED.
by Michael Sullivan

FUNDAMENTALS OF LIBRARY INSTRUCTION
by Monty L. McAdoo

FUNDAMENTALS OF LIBRARY SUPERVISION, 2ND ED.
by Joan Giesecke and Beth McNeil

FUNDAMENTALS OF MANAGING REFERENCE COLLECTIONS
by Carol A. Singer

FUNDAMENTALS OF REFERENCE
by Carolyn M. Mulac

FUNDAMENTALS OF TECHNICAL SERVICES MANAGEMENT
by Sheila S. Intner, with Peggy Johnson

SMALL PUBLIC LIBRARY MANAGEMENT
by Jane Pearlmutter and Paul Nelson

ALA FUNDAMENTALS SERIES

Fundamentals of Technical Services

John Sandstrom and Liz Miller

An imprint of the American Library Association

Chicago   2015

JOHN SANDSTROM is the Acquisitions Librarian at the New Mexico State University Library. At various times he has worked in technical services, branch management, and administration in academic, public, and special libraries, and library education. He received a Master of Library and Information Science from the University of Oklahoma, a Master of Public Administration from The University of Texas at El Paso, and is currently working on a doctorate in Education Leadership and Administration at New Mexico State University.

LIZ MILLER is the Cataloging Librarian at the New Mexico State University Library. She has written and presented workshops about practical aspects of *Resource Description and Access* (RDA). She earned her Master of Library and Information Science at the University of Wisconsin–Milwaukee. She served as President of the OLAC (Online Audiovisual Catalogers) from 2013 to 2014.

© 2015 by the American Library Association

Printed in the United States of America

19 18 17 16 15   5 4 3 2 1

Extensive effort has gone into ensuring the reliability of the information in this book; however, the publisher makes no warranty, express or implied, with respect to the material contained herein.

ISBN: 978-1-55570-966-2 (paper)

Library of Congress Cataloging-in-Publication Data

Sandstrom, John, author.
    Fundamentals of technical services / John Sandstrom and Liz Miller.
       pages   cm. — (ALA fundamentals series)
    Includes bibliographical references and index.
    ISBN 978-1-55570-966-2
    1. Technical services (Libraries) I. Miller, Liz, 1958- author. II. Title.
    Z688.5.S36 2015
    025'.02—dc23   2015011083

Cover image © kentoh/Shutterstock, Inc. Text composition in the Melior and Din typefaces by Dianne M. Rooney.

♾ This paper meets the requirements of ANSI/NISO Z39.48-1992 (Permanence of Paper).

ALA Neal-Schuman purchases fund advocacy, awareness, and accreditation programs for library professionals worldwide.

Contents

Acknowledgments

I would like to acknowledge my parents, Dave and Eve Sandstrom, for showing me it is never too late to pursue a dream; Ellen Bosman for the support she has given me throughout this project; and my coauthor, Liz Miller, for stepping in mid-project and taking on the cataloging and authority control chapters.

John Sandstrom

I want to thank my coauthor John Sandstrom for offering me this opportunity; Ellen Bosman for encouraging me and granting release time for writing; and Paula Johnson, for always being there for me.

Liz Miller

Both of us wish to acknowledge the support and help of our editors, Rachel Chance, Angela Gwizdala, and Helayne Beavers.

Introduction

Why This Book?

This book was inspired by several trends and issues that are becoming more apparent in libraries of all types. These include:

- limited resources that result in the reassignment of library staff
- reassessment of what level of staff is needed for various job functions
- increased levels of vendor-provided services and outsourcing of technical services functions
- changing standards for technical services
- changing expectations of technical services departments
- changes in library science education at all levels

For many years, when a library needed additional staff and there was no funding for new positions, staff were reassigned from technical services to other areas of the library. This has resulted in technical services departments that once were staffed with several professionals, and many more paraprofessionals, being cut down to one—or even no—professional staff, and fewer paraprofessionals.

At the same time, the advent of shared catalogs and online resources has made it easier for paraprofessionals and clerical staff to handle the bread-and-butter tasks of the technical services department. The amount of original cataloging being done by most libraries has dropped sharply over the past thirty years, and has shifted to more copy cataloging. In addition, it is getting progressively easier to find high-quality records, which makes even copy cataloging much easier.

Another contributing factor is that vendors are increasingly offering ways to move technical services functions out of the library and into their shops. These run the gamut from Patron Driven Acquisitions/Demand Driven Acquisitions (PDA/DDA), auto-ship programs, and customized cataloging, to fully processed shelf-ready materials delivered to the library's doorstep. There is a price for these services, but they can free up technical services staff to work in other areas of the library or on special projects.

There has also been a change in what's expected from technical services departments. As with many other groups, these departments are now required to do more, do it faster, and do it with fewer resources. Acquisitions units have more bibliographic information to work from, but a much smaller window during which to do this work, because titles go out of print more quickly. In cataloging, because more high-quality records are available, quirky local practices are being phased out in many libraries. As with everything else, libraries are faced with, "Do it fast, do it cheap, or do it right: choose two." Too often the decision is to go with the two measurable outcomes: fast and cheap. This has resulted in lower standards and—if your library has the resources—more time spent fixing things on the back end. Far too often, mistakes are simply ignored.

These factors have all led to changes in the expectations of what technical services departments should accomplish. It used to be that technical services staff needed to be able to research and locate desired titles; purchase them from multiple vendors, often in multiple countries; catalog them correctly for their library; physically process them; and get them on the shelf in a timely fashion. Today, thanks to globalization, market consolidation, shared cataloging, online catalogs, additional vendor services, and changing standards, technical services staff have better tools to achieve the same ends faster. This means that they must also administer online resources, including books, serials, and databases; work with or administer Electronic Resources Management Systems (ERMSs), federated search systems, and discovery systems; handle remote access issues both inside and outside of the library; and execute a host of other added duties that require just as high a level of training as more traditional job duties, all while continuing to perform most of the traditional technical services tasks. We hope that this book can help new technical services staff, whatever their level of responsibility, better understand how to fulfill all these expectations.

The final issue that compelled us to write this book comes from library education. At the graduate level, less time is being spent on technical services, with many programs only offering one required course on information organization or cataloging. This is not surprising, given the amount and variety of information needed by contemporary librarians, but it does make it difficult if you are right out of library school and asked to build a materials budget, or are expected to sit down and start cataloging on your first day as the new original cataloger. There really is no book geared to introduce the nuts and bolts of technical services to an undergraduate student, or a degreed librarian who suddenly finds himself in a technical services unit for the first time in his career.

Who This Book Is For

This book is aimed at two audiences: undergraduate students pursuing degrees in library science, and professionals and paraprofessional library staff who are moving to technical services with no prior experience.

For undergraduate students, this book will provide a clear introduction and guide to the various areas of the technical services, and describe how the parts fit together. We hope you will become comfortable with some of the terms and concepts used in technical services.

For practitioners at any level who are transitioning to technical services, we hope to give you an understanding of how technical services fits into the library as a whole, provide an overview of the area, and introduce you to the vocabulary and concepts that you will need to succeed in your new position.

Resources in This Book

We have designed this book to be used both as a textbook for use in a class or for independent study, or as a resource guide. When readers have a specific question, they can go directly to the section of the book that will give them the answer. Each chapter includes a list of resources you can consult for more information. We have also included an extensive glossary and index.

The Roadmap

If you have looked at the table of contents, you will note that this book is arranged somewhat like a technical services department's workflow. There are chapters on management, systems, collection development, acquisitions, cataloging, physical processing, authority control/catalog maintenance, and collection management. As shown in figure I.1, this mirrors the workflow of many technical services departments: materials are selected, ordered, received, cataloged, and finally processed. Authority control/catalog maintenance and collection management fall outside the basic workflow. We hope that by following this logical step-by-step process we will be able to demystify technical services.

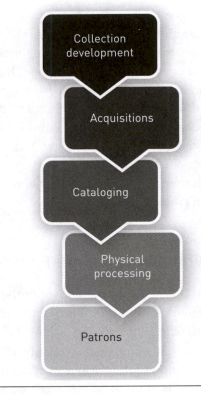

FIGURE I.1
Basic workflow—technical services

What This Book Isn't

Now that we have talked about what this book is, we want to say a few words about what this book is not. It is not an introduction to the administration of technical services departments. Although we have included a chapter addressing management at a high level, for a more complete introduction we suggest reading *Fundamentals of Technical Services Management* by Sheila Intner with Peggy Johnson.[1]

This is also not a guide or textbook for collection development, acquisitions, cataloging, or physical processing. It is only an introduction. Entire books have been written on each of these functional areas. We provide some of those titles in the lists of resources at the end of each chapter.

Finally, this book is not is a series of best practices. Libraries have a long and rich history of solving problems using means designed to suit their unique cultures and the requirements placed on them by funding agencies and other stakeholders. A best practice at one library may be completely unrealistic at another.

Final Thoughts

As you use this book—either by working through it from front to back or dipping into it for help and guidance when you have a question—we hope that we have contributed to your understanding of a rarely seen but critical part of the library.

NOTE

1. Sheila Intner with Peggy Johnson. *Fundamentals of Technical Services Management* (Chicago: American Library Association, 2008).

1

Managing Technical Services

There are many skills needed to manage any organization, and the technical services department requires all of them. These include budgeting, purchasing, human resources management, computer systems, time management, and project management, in addition to all the other skills needed to be a librarian. Technical services is a bit different from other departments of the library, because its customers are primarily internal, although the services it provides also directly affect library users. This chapter gives a high-level overview of some core issues and concerns (see the list of resources at the end of the chapter for publications that address the topic in detail). In addition to discussing the typical organizational structure of technical services departments, this overview covers two critical areas for management: communication and workflow.

This chapter will cover:

- Organization of technical services departments
- Communication
- Workflows
- Trends and issues in managing technical services

Before You Begin

Before you begin, you will need to collect and read the policies regarding your library's technical services department and its subunits. These documents include information critical to the effective and efficient management of your department. If you aren't the manager, this will help you to understand where technical services fits into the big picture of the library. Unfortunately, in many cases you may find that these policies either don't exist, or are so out of date as to be unusable. If this is the case, you may need to start documenting everything you find to contribute to a new policy. At the same time, don't ignore any procedural documents you find. Procedures are often included in other policy documents, even if these serve different purposes. *How* a department does something (procedure) can be just as important as *why* the department does it (policy).

Specialized Terms

Budget—The monetary resources available to an institution for the support of their programs. Budgeting is the process of allocating a budget based on those resources.

Communication—At its most basic, the sharing of information.

Computer systems—Each institution uses a variety of computer systems, ranging from stand-alone personal computers to large networks.

Human resources management—Back in the day, this was called *personnel.* This is the unit that is responsible for coordinating the staff resources available to an institution.

Policy—A document, or set of documents, that describes the principles, rules, and guidelines formulated by the library to reach its long-term goals.

Procedure—A document, or set of documents, that describes how the activities of the library or subunit are carried out.

Project management—A specialized set of skills that is used to organize and coordinate complicated projects involving multiple departments.

Purchasing—The process of buying materials and supplies for the institution. The department responsible for this is often called the *purchasing unit.*

Time management—The conflict between what you need to accomplish and the resources you have available to do it. Allocating and tracking how much time you and your staff spend on each duty is essential.

Workflow—The movement of activities into, through, and out of a series of processes.

Organization of Technical Services Departments

One factor that affects both communications and workflow is how the library and the technical services department are organized. The organization dictates how work flows into and out of the technical services department, and with whom the manager of the department works most closely.

The technical services department manager must maintain a dual focus. She must look internally to examine the department to make sure everything is functioning smoothly, and also externally to ensure that other library departments and the general public receives the services they need from technical services. In many libraries, the technical services department manager serves as the backup for all technical services positions, and so must be able to perform any job she supervises.

As with any group, the more people involved, the more complicated the organization becomes. This is particularly true of technical services. In small libraries with minimal staff, everything discussed in this book might be the responsibility of a single person. In large libraries with greater numbers of staff, technical services may be made up of dozens of people.

In general, technical services departments break down into four areas or units: collection development, acquisitions, cataloging, and physical processing. The exact duties of each unit and in what order they are performed will vary by library, but generally tend to be fairly linear, as shown by the organization chart in figure 1.1.

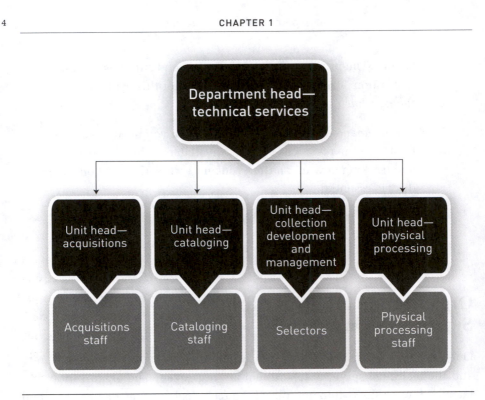

FIGURE 1.1

Sample organization chart for technical services

Staffing

The more people employed in the technical services department, the more types of positions there will be. Most departments will have at least one degreed librarian (a person with a master's degree in library science), para-professionals (staff members with higher levels of experience or education, or both), clerks, and assistants. However, small libraries may have a single non-degreed person doing everything, while the largest libraries will have multiple degreed librarians at a variety of levels.

Communication

At its most basic, communication is the sharing of information. Managing communication is therefore managing how information is shared, which can occur by means ranging from very formal to very informal. Both formal and informal methods play a role when communicating among different parts of the library community, including vendors, staff, and patrons. However, each has its pitfalls, too. These can result because of differing priorities, lack of understanding, and sometimes just plain personality conflicts. As a member of a complicated organization like a library, it is important to be aware of and adept at several types of communication.

Internal

There are two types of internal communication for most technical services departments: internal to the department and internal to the library. Each type has specific characteristics, which need to be kept in mind to avoid missteps.

Internal-to-the-department communication takes place among the various units that make up the technical services department. Collection development must communicate with acquisitions, acquisitions must communicate with cataloging, cataloging must communicate with physical processing, and so on. Often this communication is informal, consisting of "hallway meetings," as opposed to more formal types of communication such as written memos or e-mail. Regardless of its level of formality, this communication must be timely, clear, and concise. Communication can be easier in smaller departments because there are fewer people involved, but it is still important. If communication among various units breaks down, it is up to the supervisors of those units to takes steps to repair it as quickly as possible, which often requires shifting to more formal means of communication for the short term.

Internal-to-the-library communication takes place between technical services and the other departments of the library. Access services and public services departments need to give feedback about patron needs to technical services. Technical services must let library administration know what its needs are, and the administration must let technical services know what is expected of it. This type of communication tends to be formal, perhaps taking place at official meetings, and more hierarchical, with questions and concerns addressed to the department head and answers coming back down the chain. However, there is often an unofficial network that can be just as effective as, and sometimes faster than, the official lines of communication. Unless a library has only one or two employees, there will be an informal network that connects everyone at some level that takes place outside of the official lines of supervision or communication. It is important to be aware of these, because they are often perceived to be more trustworthy and up-to-date than the official lines of communication. Unfortunately, these "grapevines" can be very inaccurate, and the communication among the various departments of the library must be timely, clear, and concise.

External

External communication takes place among technical services and organizations outside of the library. There are two types of external groups with which technical services staff regularly communicate. These are vendors and other organizations for which the library is a customer, for example, book vendors, such as Baker & Taylor or Ingram; periodical vendors, such as Coutts or Harrassowitz; and information aggregators, such as ProQuest or EBSCO. More rarely, technical services staff will be called on to respond to library users or funding agencies, such as city governments, donors, or grant agencies.

Communicating with vendors and other groups with which the library and technical services do business can be very difficult. It is dictated by the relationship you, as the library representative, have with each vendor and its representative. These relationships can range from very formal to informal. It takes time and experience for each relationship to find its own level. One critical thing to remember is that vendors are not your enemies. A vendor may be seen as an adversary because your goal is to serve your patrons, whereas the vendor's goal is to make money. This dichotomy may cause issues and hard feelings between library staff and a vendor. Vendor representatives must obey the rules set by their company, yet they do not want to lose you as a customer. You, as the library representative, must obey the rules set by your funding agency, yet you do not want to lose access to the vendor's products and services. Ideally, your vendors will form a partnership that helps you to improve your library's services while allowing them to make a reasonable profit.

Unfortunately, some vendors lose track of the value of library partnerships, and the relationship can become exploitive. An example of this would be when a publisher has what amounts to a monopoly on a set of journals, and starts increasing prices beyond a reasonable level. In this situation, you must openly communicate your concerns and what the results will be if the exploitation continues; for example, you may reduce the amount of money you spend, or take your business elsewhere. Be assured that if you are having

issues with a particular vendor, other libraries are, too. When enough libraries take their business elsewhere, the vendor will either wake up and change,
or go out of business. An exception may be a periodicals vendor who is the
sole source for some titles or services. But even in this case, the right comments and actions may get them to change how they treat the library market
and individual libraries.

One of the common topics that vendors and libraries communicate about
is contracts and licenses. Because these are legal agreements, the rules of
your funding organization may require approval at additional levels outside
the library. When negotiating a license or contract, the library's business officer will usually need to be included, as well as staff from the purchasing
department of the funding agency. For some contracts and licenses, you may
even need to work with lawyers. This can be a challenge, because lawyers
typically don't understand how libraries work, even if they understand what
libraries do. The library staff member involved in these negotiations needs to
be ready to explain the library's operations and needs.

Another type of external communication occurs on those occasions
when funding agencies or patrons contact technical services directly. This
will most often be concerned with collection development and acquisitions,
when patrons want to know if certain titles have been ordered or received.
It is important to remember that you are representing the library. If the question is not in your area of responsibility, make sure to refer it to the appropriate person or office rather than risk responding in a way that will cause
problems for other staff. An example of this would be attempting to respond
to a question about serials management when you work with monographic
acquisitions.

Always remember that communication is a crucial part of working in any
organization, and it becomes more critical the higher you move up the chain
of command. In technical services, you must be able to communicate with
several different groups in a variety of ways. Communication may be formal
or informal, written or verbal, remote or face-to-face, so flexibility is a key skill
to develop. The way you communicate with staff in your unit is different from
how you communicate with other library staff, vendors, patrons, or representatives from funding agencies. Whether you are a supervisor or working in the
trenches, you must adjust your communication style accordingly.

In many cases, communication will take place in meetings. For some
hints on running effective meetings, please check out the sidebar.

Ten Tips for Running an Efficient and Effective Meeting

1. **Schedule as far in advance as possible.** Calendars fill up quickly, so the earlier you schedule meetings, the less rearranging participants have to do.

2. **Only invite the people who must be there.** Inviting people who don't need to be at a meeting wastes your time and theirs.

3. **Have a written agenda.** This allows the person who calls the meeting to define what the meeting is about and to keep it on track.

4. **Don't try to do too much at one meeting.** One hour is about the limit for a productive meeting. Beyond that, people begin to lose focus and stop paying attention.

5. **Send the agenda out early.** This gives the attendees the opportunity to see what the meeting is about and prepare for it.

6. **Send relevant documents and background information out with the agenda.** If there is information that participants need to review prior to the meeting, make sure it goes out in a timely fashion.

7. **Be organized.** Make sure that you are prepared for the meeting and have all the information you expect to need.

8. **Start the meeting on time.** Those attending have made time to attend the meeting. Don't waste it by starting late.

9. **Keep it focused.** Make sure to keep the meeting focused on the agenda items. Don't allow it to be side-railed into other issues that attendees may or may not be prepared to discuss.

10. **End on time.** The participants are as busy people as you. Make sure you end the meeting on time so that everyone can get on with their days.

And here is a bonus!

11. **Follow up.** Send everyone a document that clearly reports what decisions were made, what action items need to be addressed, and who is responsible for each action item.

Workflows

One of the most critical things to understand when managing any type of operation is workflow. Understanding the organization's workflow allows a manager to plan for the most efficient and effective management of resources, including staff, materials, and time. This understanding can guide reorganizations, personnel planning, needs forecasting, cost-benefit analysis, and budget justification, as well as providing a host of other information that other parts of the library's operation may need.

This book includes series of very high-level workflows that review what each unit of the technical services department is responsible for and the major steps in the workflow of each area. If and when you need to build a workflow chart for an existing unit, you can include as much detail as you need to. It can be built as a chart, a narrative, or a combination of the two, depending on the audience and how the document is to be used.

There are several ways to build a workflow document, so tailor the methodology to the audience, level of formality, and complexity of the organization. If it is a high-level document, then the unit manager or the manager of technical services can probably build it for herself. This will result in a fairly simple document similar to those shown in this book. If a very detailed workflow is required, each person in the department will need to document the workflow for each of the tasks he or she is involved in. Building this type of detailed workflow requires a huge investment of time and energy, but it gives the manager the information she needs to really understand what is happening in her unit or department.

Charting workflows is especially good for identifying issues in the current workflow of the department or unit. Almost every department has activities that are not really necessary, or that would be handled more efficiently if moved to a different part of the workflow. Detailed charting that goes to the individual staff level will allow those activities to be easily identified, and either shifted or eliminated as appropriate.

Another useful result of workflow charting is that it creates a document that explains exactly what the technical services department does. Unfortunately, in many libraries, technical services is tucked away behind the scenes, and most of the public services staff—and even library administrators—don't have a clear understanding of what the department does. A detailed and

annotated workflow chart should explain what technical services does in
terms that even a person who is not part of the library can understand.

Trends and Issues in Managing Technical Services

As with all managers in the library, technical services managers are expected
to do more with less. As formats change and the needs of our patrons continue to evolve, the process of managing technical services will also evolve
and change. Two major trends have emerged.

The first is flexibility. Management in technical services must be
extremely flexible to be able to integrate new workflows or change existing workflows very quickly. New products, services, and opportunities are
becoming available almost every day. Flexibility and open-mindedness are
critical for taking advantage of them.

The second is the trend towards outsourcing, or contracting with a company outside the library to provide certain services. Although this will be
discussed in more depth later in this book, it would be remiss not to mention
it here. The decision whether or not to outsource a function in technical services is, at its heart, a management decision. There is no single answer that
will apply to all libraries.

Final Thoughts

This chapter has reviewed some of the basics of managing the technical services department of a library. These include organization, communication,
workflows, and trends and issues. Try to keep the issues discussed here in
mind as you work through the rest of this book, because they affect everything that is done in technical services in one way or another. As with all
parts of the library, technical services departments are changing very rapidly.
The better you understand and document your department's organization
and processes, the easier it will be to change them if necessary.

Resources

Canepi, Kitti. "Work Analysis in Library Technical Services." *Technical Services Quarterly* 25, no. 2 (2007): 19–30.

Intner, Sheila, with Peggy Johnson. *Fundamentals of Library Technical Services Management.* Chicago: American Library Association, 2008.

Jurard, Susan, and Susan Barnard. *Integrating Total Quality Management in a Library Setting.* New York: Routledge, 2013.

Wilson, K. A. "Library Technical Services Outsourcing: A Select Bibliography." 1997. www.ala.org/Template.cfm?Section=outsourcing&Template=/ContentManagement/ContentDisplay.cfm&ContentID=42931.

Systems

Technical services uses several different types of computer-based systems. These generally fall into four categories: Integrated Library Systems, Electronic Resources Management Systems, discovery services, and Electronic Data Interfaces. Although these may be stand-alone systems, they are often tied together through various communication protocols so they can easily exchange information. This chapter will review what each type of system is, how it is used, and how it fits together with other systems to support technical services.

This chapter will cover:

- Integrated Library Systems
- Electronic Resources Management Systems
- Discovery services
- Electronic Data Interfaces
- Trends and issues in systems

Before You Begin

Before you begin working with the different types of systems that are part of technical services, there are a few things you need to determine:

- What systems are you using?
- Which company provides your ILS and who at your library is responsible for maintaining it?

- Do you have an ERMS? If so, who is responsible for it?
- Who is responsible for your Internet connectivity?
- Which budget pays for all this?

You also need to know the policies and procedures that govern the selection and use of these systems.

Specialized Terms

Formatting—A means of encoding data for storage.

Importing/exporting—Ways of moving data in/out of a set of tables.

Module—Part of a larger program that focuses on one specialized area.

Protocol—An agreement between two or more groups to use the same communications format.

Queries—Programmed questions used to report on a data set.

Reports—Data retrieved from the system for specific purposes.

Tables—A way to store data.

Integrated Library Systems

Integrated Library Systems (ILSs) are, in many respects, the computer systems that hold the entire library together. They are made up of multiple modules and submodules, which may include:

- Acquisitions
- Cataloging
- Circulation
- Reference
- Online Public Access Catalog
- Reporting

For the library to run efficiently and effectively, all the modules need to be in constant communication with each other. Each module includes a series of data tables arranged and linked by certain variables that allow all of its data to be accessed at different times by different modules for different reasons. The ILS is, basically, a huge database that includes the entire history of each item in the library.

The modules used most in technical services are acquisitions, cataloging, and reporting. The technical services department usually doesn't need to use the circulation, public access catalog, or reference modules.

The *acquisitions module* is where the order information for an item is input and tracked. It handles the fund accounting for the materials budget, and tracks invoices and payments to and from each vendor. In some systems, the acquisitions module also has collection development functionality that allows selection lists to be developed and ordered from within the ILS.

The *cataloging module* adds to the information created in the acquisitions module by upgrading bibliographic records and adding information on holdings and ownership that is needed by the circulation module. It also has specialized features that allow it to import and export records from bibliographic utilities such as OCLC. The cataloging module is also where the information needed for labeling materials is added to the record.

The *Online Public Access Catalog* (OPAC) is the module that provides the interface between the ILS and the public. It is important for both acquisitions and cataloging to watch this module and to ensure that it formats the data they provide in a way the public can understand. Because the format can change unexpectedly due to operating system upgrades, ILS upgrades, or a number of other reasons, it is necessary to make sure the records are displaying correctly, and to fix any problems that show up in a timely fashion.

The *reporting module* allows staff to pull data from various tables to compose the reports needed to administer the library. This information can include everything from patron demographics to the average age of the collection or the average time it takes a vendor to fulfill its orders. Although most ILSs come with some canned (pre-written) reports, a database programming language may be required to write customized reports. This can be done via a third-party report writer, or by writing custom report routines. Structured Query Language (SQL), one of the most common programming languages used for report writing, is used by Microsoft Access and many other database programs. A firm grounding in this or one of the other programming languages used for report writing enhances your ability to develop the specialized reports needed by your organization.

Electronic Resources Management Systems

Electronic Resources Management Systems (ERMSs) are specialized systems used to track information about the electronic resources the library has access to. This information includes licensing, subscription dates, access dates, access URLs, vendor support, user names, passwords, and any other information needed to access and administer the library's electronic resources. An ERMS also generally includes the ability to aggregate and report usage statistics for the products they track, which makes it a critical tool for evaluating the effectiveness of an electronic resources collection. As more of the library acquisitions process moves to electronic formats, the ERMS has become increasingly important to the administration of electronic resources. It is tied very closely to the ILS and acts as a gateway from the ILS to the library's electronic resources, which may or may not reside on a local server. Some examples of ERMSs are Innovative Interfaces' Content Access Service (CASE) and ProQuest's 360 Resource Manager.

Discovery Services

A discovery service is either an integrated module of the ILS or a third-party product that creates a single searchable index of all, or almost all, of a library's accessible content. This includes physical materials owned by the library, as well as those online resources accessible to the library. Discovery services are important to technical services because the information they draw on to create the central index is maintained and updated by different units within technical services. Depending on the organization of the library, technical services staff may also use discovery modules for searching or maintaining a number of systems.

Electronic Data Interfaces

An Electronic Data Interface (EDI) is not technically a system, but rather a critical protocol that connects all the various computer systems used in the library and allows them to communicate with each other and with systems outside the library. EDI allows large groups of records to be imported into the catalog from bibliographic utilities, and fulfillment data to be shared between vendors and the library.

EDI protocols are useful because they save time and paper—and thereby save money—for both the library and the vendor. If you have not implemented EDI, you may want to check with your business office to see if your current business model will allow exchanging information with vendors electronically. Although implementation can require changes to your business practices, the savings realized through greater efficiency will generally make up for the costs of making the changes.

EDI is controlled by various standards that have been developed by national and international standard-making bodies. These include the American National Standards Institute (ANSI) and the United Nations rules for Electronic Data Interchange for Administration, Commerce and Transport (UN/EDIFACT).

Trends and Issues in Systems

In the early days of library automation, a library might have contracted with multiple companies to provide the different modules it needed. As the industry consolidated, the ILSs in use today were developed. The current trend is to combine ERMS, ILS, EDI, and discovery services to form a "next-generation ILS," also called a Library Services Platform (LSP), which can handle all of a library's needs as well as those of its patrons. Examples of next-generation ILSs are Ex Libris's Alma, OCLC's Worldshare Management Services, and Innovative Interfaces' Sierra. One consideration with these services is whether or not they work well with products from other vendors; for example, a discovery service may not work well with an e-book provider's platform.

Final Thoughts

Systems are critical to library technical services. Every technical services unit interfaces with multiple systems every day. A thorough understanding of those systems is important for the smooth functioning of technical services, even if the systems are administered by different departments of the library.

Resources

Antell, Karen, Molly Strothmann, Dianne Cmor, and Rory Litwin. "Should We Retire the Catalog?" *Reference & User Services Quarterly* 53, no. 3 (Spring 2014): 213–216.

Banoun, Susan, Deberah England, Sharon Purtee, Angela Riggio, and Becky Schwartzkopf. "ERM Systems and Impact on Technical Services." *Serials Librarian* 60 (2011): 135–140.

Bilal, Diana. *Library Automation: Core Concepts and Practical Systems Analysis.* Santa Barbara: Libraries Unlimited, 2014.

Collins, Maria, and Jill E. Grogg. "Building a Better ERMS." *Library Journal* 136, no. 4 (March 2011): 22–28.

Djenno, Mireille, Glenda Insua, Gwen M. Gregory, and John S. Brantley. "Discovering Usability: Comparing Two Discovery Systems at One Academic Library." *Journal of Web Librarianship* 8, no. 3 (2014): 263–285.

Feick, Tina, and Donna Packer. "EDI (Electronic Data Interchange) for Libraries, Publishers, and Agents: The Reality Show—SUSHI, ONIX and ?" *Serials Librarian* 54, no. 3–4 (2008): 261–264.

Mihlrad, Leigh. "A Brief Introduction to ERMS." *Journal of Electronic Resources in Medical Libraries* 7, no. 2 (2010): 151–158.

Roach, Dani, and Sharon Dyas-Correia. "Moving Mountains of Cost Data: Standards for ILS to ERM System to Vendors and Back Again." *Serials Librarian* 58, no. 1–4 (2010): 198–203.

3

Collection Development

Collection development is the process of choosing which materials to add to the library. Although this sounds fairly straightforward (see figure 3.1) it can be difficult for a variety of reasons, notably because collection development may be part of public services or acquisitions, a separate unit in technical services, or a freestanding department. Because it is fairly common to find combined collection development/acquisitions positions, collection development is treated as the beginning of the technical services workflow.

Collection development is complicated by the variety of criteria that can be used for selecting materials. These criteria can be as basic as "We will add all titles that appear on the *New York Times* Best Sellers list," or they may be more complex criteria that are based on subject matter, publication date, publisher, author, geographical coverage, format, and any number of other variables determined by library staff.

Selection criteria will also vary depending on which part of the collection they address. The criteria used for adult fiction will differ from those used

FIGURE 3.1
Basic workflow— collection development

for juvenile fiction, periodicals, audiovisual materials, reference, electronic materials, and so forth. Documenting these criteria and keeping them up-to-date can seem like a full-time job. Ideally, all the criteria used by the library should be gathered together in the collection development policy.

This chapter will cover:

- Modes of issuance
- One-time-purchase materials (monographs)
- Materials purchased on an ongoing basis
    Serials
    Integrating resources
- Trends and issues in collection development

Before You Begin

Most libraries have a collection development policy in place. *Read it!* Get to know it. It is an invaluable guide to determining the collection needs of your library, and how they have been fulfilled in the past. This policy defines what the library collects and details the criteria used for making selection decisions. The responsibility for developing and maintaining this policy will vary according to who at your library is in charge of collection development and selection. In general, it is done by the selector(s), in coordination with whomever is in charge of collection development. In larger systems, this may be a committee, while in smaller systems it may be a single person.

The collection development policy will help guide you through how your institution performs collection development and selection. In addition to reading it, you should ask staff how it is being implemented. It is a sad fact that the policies and procedures of many libraries have not kept up with current practice. If your policy, procedure, and practice do not align, it is critical to update it.

If you are opening a new library, congratulations! You get to write the collection development policy and decide how it will be implemented at your library. Although the process of writing policies won't be discussed here, there are some good resources included in the list of readings at the end of the chapter.

In general, the collection development policy should include the following elements:

- which part of the collection the policy applies to (for example, adult fiction, electronic resources, homework help, etc.)
- the mode of issuance of the collection
- the criteria being used to select materials for the collection

It is also helpful to have a formal statement describing a review cycle for the policy. This may appear in the collection development policy, or may be defined in another part of the library's policy manual.

Specialized Terms

Aggregator—A company that brings together information from several sources and indexes in ways that make it more accessible to users.

Annual—Materials that are published on an annual basis and automatically ordered as serials.

Budget—The amount of money available for a particular function, in this case the materials budget.

Integrating resource—A resource in which some parts change from time to time, while leaving the resource as a whole essentially the same. An electronic integrating resource exists in an online or digital format.

Monograph—Originally used to describe physical books, the term *monograph* has expanded to include a resource that is complete in one part or a definite number of parts, regardless of format.

Provider—A general term used for companies that provide information, which can often be equated with *publisher*.

Serial—A publication issued over time in distinct parts, with each part bearing the same title, regardless of format.

Standing order—A resource that is published on an irregular basis and automatically ordered as a serial.

Modes of Issuance

Libraries primarily collect published materials that are mass-produced and widely disseminated. There are four different ways materials can be issued by a publisher:

A *monograph* is a resource that is complete in one part or a definite number of parts. The most familiar example of a monograph is a printed book; for example, the paperback edition of *The Hunger Games* is a monograph. However, not all monographs are printed or text-based. An e-book version of *To Kill a Mockingbird*, a roadmap of Minnesota, the CD *Court and Spark* by Joni Mitchell, and a DVD of the movie *Little Miss Sunshine* are all monographs.

A *serial* is a publication issued over time in distinct parts, with each part having the same title. In addition, a serial is published with no predetermined end date. The parts of a serial are usually published at regular intervals and are numbered and/or dated, but this is not always the case. For example, *People* magazine is a serial. Each issue of *People* has the same title, but its content is different from other issues. A new issue is published every week, and the publishers intend to keep publishing the magazine indefinitely. Another example of a serial is a newspaper. Some serials are more difficult to identify. For example, *The World Almanac and Book of Facts 2015* resembles a book, but since it has the same title year after year, is issued in distinct parts, has a different date on each issue, and seems like it will be published indefinitely, it is usually considered a serial. All issues of a serial are cataloged on a single record in the library's online catalog.

An *integrating resource*, like a serial, is published over time. However, instead of being made up of distinct parts, some parts of the resource occasionally change, with the resource as a whole essentially remaining the same. For example, the website for radio station KCRW (www.kcrw.com) is frequently updated, but the parts that are updated are *integrated* into the website. Another example of an integrating resource is an updating looseleaf publication. The resource is kept in a binder so pages can be easily added and removed. The publisher periodically sends updated pages with instructions on how they should be filed to replace outdated pages. The entire resource remains essentially the same, but some information has been changed.

A *series* is a group of related but separately published works issued over time by the same publisher. Although each work that makes up the series has its own title, it also bears the title of the series, and sometimes a number. For example, *The 39 Clues* is the title of a series of children's books. *Vespers Rising* is the eleventh book in the series, which in addition to its own title has "The 39 Clues, Book Eleven" printed on the cover. *Vespers Rising* would have its own record in the library catalog; the record would include the series title, *The 39 Clues*, and the words "book eleven." Although most series are handled as groups of individual titles, they may also be handled like serials, with a single catalog record for the entire series. An example of this is *The Old Farmer's Almanac*, which is published once a year. Each year's *Old Farmer's Almanac* could have its own record in the catalog, or the entire series could be represented by one catalog record. For collection development purposes, serials can be treated as either a group of monographs or as a serial, depending on how they are cataloged in the ILS.

Selectors may use different criteria and methods for choosing materials for each mode of issuance. A review of the steps required for the different types—one-time-purchase materials (monographs), serials, and integrating resources—follows.

Monographs

One-time-purchase materials, or monographs, include most books (all bindings and e-books), DVDs, Blu-ray discs, CDs, and any other materials that only need to be purchases once. This does not include serials (e.g., periodicals or magazines) or other content that is subscribed to for a specific period of time (e.g., access to databases or aggregators). There are four basic steps to identifying which titles you would like to add to a collection. These are:

1. Identify the publication universe.
2. Select the items to request.

3. Determine the budget.

4. Make the request.

STEP 1: Identify the Publication Universe

The publishing universe is made up of hundreds of thousands of titles, which may or may not be available for purchase by libraries. These range from self-published works to one-time monographs to new e-editions of old classics. Sorting through all these materials to find the gems you want to add to your collection could itself be the subject of several books. Although this won't be discussed in great detail here, a few ways of making the process manageable are discussed below.

Before you begin reviewing titles for inclusion in your collection, it's necessary to limit the publication universe to the titles that will be of interest to your library's patrons. For example, if you are selecting for a public library, you don't need to look at most of the body of academic publishing. Conversely, if you are working at an academic institution, you don't need to review materials unrelated to the academic programs at your institution.

There are a number of variables that can be used to narrow the publication universe. Many of these are based on easily available data. These include:

- publisher/producer
- publication date
- subject
- audience
- reviews
- format
- price

Identifying and choosing *publishers* and *producers* that create the types of materials you want to request allows you to narrow your focus. For example, you wouldn't need to look at the product list of an academic publisher if you are looking for children's books. If you want to request popular DVDs, you probably don't need to see the titles produced by a school media company.

Publication dates are important if you want to look for just the newest materials, fill in gaps from the past five years, or look for publications dates in a particular bracket of years.

Limiting the publication universe by *subject* is a convenient way to shrink the number of titles you review. However, this can also be difficult because publishers, vendors, and libraries all handle subjects a bit differently. Be careful to make sure you know exactly what types of subjects you use to limit. Publishers and or vendors have been known to assign subjects in such a way as to get a title into the segment of the retail market where they believe it will sell best. This doesn't always match how a library would assign subject headings. The Library of Congress assigns authoritative subject headings based on the *Library of Congress Subject Headings*, but other libraries may assign additional subject headings based on *Sears Subject Headings* or another subject heading scheme. However, there are also materials (e.g., most audiovisual materials) that the Library of Congress and other sources of cataloging do not handle, which has led to a variety of "homegrown" subject lists for these materials.

Audience describes the interest group an item is written for. Examples of this include juvenile, academic, historical, and biographical. This is useful when you need an adult popular treatment of a subject rather than an item more appropriate for juvenile patrons. Audience can be suggested by the authors, publishers, and retailers.

Reviews are another source of information. Not everything that is published is reviewed in a standard source. Limiting your publication universe to only those materials that have been reviewed will help narrow the number of titles you examine. You can further limit by where an item was reviewed, or even how many times it was reviewed. However, this should not be your only consideration, because there are many good and worthwhile materials out there that are either not reviewed or are not reviewed in a timely fashion. This is typically a limiter that you work with your vendor to develop.

Many libraries define up front what *formats* they do and do not collect. For example, many libraries do not collect mass-market paperbacks in their cataloged collection. Most no longer collect VHS tapes even if they still have a small collection of them on the shelf. Other libraries that have a preference for e-books may build specific lists of just those titles. Limiting by format early in the process can save you time by excluding formats that you know you won't order.

Limiting by *price* can be difficult because materials in different selection areas may have very different average prices. For example, setting a $25 cap for adult nonfiction won't work for art books, which are typically priced at $50 or more. But if you can be flexible about how you use it, price can be a very powerful limiter for including or excluding a title on your list.

You can use almost any other factor you wish to include or exclude materials from your lists. About the only limit is the flexibility of the system you are using. Work with your vendor reps and don't be afraid to spend time experimenting with the system. The important thing to remember is that sometimes a small change can lead to big results. For example, changing a date limiter can change the number of titles either included or excluded by several hundred.

There are a variety of tools that can help you limit the number of titles you need to examine. These can automatically cut out those titles that do not meet your basic criteria. Most of these tools have been developed by various vendors (e.g., Baker & Taylor's Title Source, Ingram's ipage, or Yankee Book Peddler's GOBI). Vendors will make their systems available to you, and may even provide selection lists based on any criteria that they track. An advantage of vendor pre-selection of this type is that the vendor does the work of finding the titles that fit your criteria. A disadvantage of this method is that it can become more difficult to locate the occasional crossover title that a patron may request.

Approval Plans and Demand (or Patron) Driven Acquisitions

Approval plans and Demand (or Patron) Driven Acquisitions (DDA/PDA) are ways of getting the materials you need without spending as much staff time acquiring them. Approval plans are designed primarily for physical books, while DDA/PDA programs are used for e-books. They have similar advantages and disadvantages.

Approval and DDA/PDA plans are both profile-based ways of finding the materials that you want to add to your library. Profiles are documents, created collaboratively between your library's collection development staff and your vendors, which describe what kinds of materials the library needs. Profiles can include subjects, publication dates, audiences, and publishers. In the case of approval plans, your vendor will send you books that match your profile on a regular basis. You have a set amount of time to review the books and choose which ones to keep and which ones to send back. Ideally, you will keep far more books than you return.

In DDA/PDA programs, the vendors will provide access to their e-book collections that match your profile. Records for these selected e-books are loaded into your catalog for easier discovery by your patrons. The e-books

Another way of limiting the publication universe is to simply have patrons and staff request those titles they need or want. This is one style of Patron Driven Acquisitions that can be used in conjunction with regular selection by library staff, or as the basis of your entire collection development system. An advantage here is that most materials requested this way will get used at least once. However, it requires a fair amount of active administration to limit unintended duplication and to ensure balanced development of different parts of the collection.

STEP 2: Select the Items to Request

In general, there are four different ways of choosing what to request from the materials that remain after narrowing your view of the publishing universe. These are *distributed selection, semi-centralized selection, centralized*

available are updated on a regular basis as new titles are published and some titles become unavailable for a variety of possible reasons, from being superseded to a change in the publisher's agreement with the vendor. Each time a title is checked out, the library is charged a certain percentage of the list price for the short-term loan (STL). When a predetermined number of loans is reached, the library automatically buys the book.

Both approval plans and DDA/PDA programs have the advantage of being fairly low-maintenance once they are set up. They also allow you to commit a set amount of money to a vendor and then not think about it again until it is almost spent. They will also help you to keep up with current publications.

However, these programs have several disadvantages. Selectors have little input beyond the profiling level. In approval plans, the regular process of receiving new titles and shipping back those that aren't selected requires staff time and effort. Approval plans and DDA/PDA programs have high set-up costs because of the staff time required to develop the library's profile and to add large numbers of records to the library's catalog. Staff time must also be invested in the ongoing maintenance of adding new titles and removing those that are no longer available. The greatest disadvantage is potentially having to pay for each STL in addition to the purchase price of the book.

These types of programs are a good choice for many, but not all, libraries so investigate carefully before deciding to adopt an approval or DDA/PDA plan.

selection, and *outsourced selection*. Each of these is appropriate in different situations and has its own set of advantages and disadvantages.

DISTRIBUTED SELECTION

Distributed selection involves item-by-item selection performed independently by selectors working on behalf of the library. Depending on the type of library, selectors may be staff or users. They may be formal groups, such as a reader's advisory group, or an informal group that works together on a more ad hoc basis.

- Selection is done by those with the best knowledge of library needs.
- Staff buy-in is increased.

Disadvantages of distributed selection include:

- The possibility of little or no coordination among the people or groups doing selection.
- It can be difficult to ensure that basic needs are not overlooked.
- Requests may be duplicated.
- Different staff members may unknowingly duplicate each other's efforts.
- All selectors must work on the same schedule.

SEMI-CENTRALIZED SELECTION

Semi-centralized selection involves a committee made up of a limited number of representatives who gather at regular intervals to request materials on behalf of the library. This group can be made up of whomever is deemed appropriate by library administration, but usually includes representative professional and paraprofessional staff.

Advantages to semi-centralized selection include:

- More thought is given to each title.
- Fewer staff resources are needed.
- Workflow is improved because selection times are coordinated.

Disadvantages include:

- Staff must interrupt their regular duties to attend selection meetings.

- Collections are more homogeneous.
- Staff buy-in is reduced.

CENTRALIZED SELECTION

In centralized selection, dedicated staff do all the selection for the library with input from other staff or users with specialized knowledge.

Advantages of centralized selection include:

- Staff resources are used most efficiently.
- The specialized knowledge of various staff is optimized.
- Coordinating selection decisions with acquisitions unit becomes easier, because fewer staff are making those decisions.

Disadvantages include:

- Most staff are uninvolved in selection process, resulting in less buy-in to and knowledge of the collection.
- The library may be less responsive to special needs in some parts of the collection because those selecting materials may not be subject experts.

OUTSOURCED SELECTION

Outsourced selection has been used with varying degrees of success. You give a third party, either a vendor or an outside consultant, the authority to request materials on your behalf. These requests will usually be based on some type of profile describing your library and its needs.

Advantages include:

- Fewer staff resources are needed for collection development and selection.
- High-demand materials may be requested as soon as they are announced to the vendors, which ensures a faster fill rate.
- Because the expert selectors spend all their time doing selection, they are more experienced and knowledgeable in collection development.

Disadvantages include:

- Direct local control of the collection is minimal.
- Library staff are not motivated to buy into the process.

- External selectors may not be perceived as understanding what the library needs.
- Users and funders may be uneasy with the lack of local control.

Remember that whatever the method you use in your library, it is only a tool. Just as you are not limited to a single tool when you are fixing a car, it is not necessary to use a single method of selection. Different types of materials can be selected using different methods. For example, in an academic library, graduate-level materials may be selected by subject specialists and faculty through distributed selection, and undergraduate materials may be selected by a committee in a semi-centralized method. Serials may be selected by the serials librarian in a centralized method, while Spanish-language selection is outsourced through an approval plan. Each one is appropriate in its own way in its own setting.

CHOOSING THE RIGHT ITEMS

Now that we've looked at various selection methods, the question becomes, "But how do I know what to choose?" This is probably one of the most difficult parts of the selection process. Every selector has requested materials that just sit on the shelf, while other materials they've chosen have been popular with users. Or a title may have circulated heavily when it was featured in the new books area, but once it went to the regular stacks, it was never heard from again.

We've all made mistakes. You didn't order the sleeper hit of the summer, or you bought every item on the American Film Institute Top 100 list, but not one of the titles was checked out. It happens. As long as it doesn't happen too often, you don't need to worry.

Much of what is requested is based on the selector's knowledge of what has been popular or useful in the past. New selectors may unwittingly impose their own biases into the selection process. Failing to maintain objectivity can result in libraries with collections that are wildly unsuited to their patron base. Here are some examples:

- a branch library in an impoverished central city with a complete collection of fiction from the *New York Times* Best Sellers list
- a library used primarily as a small-business resource center with a large collection of art history materials

- a library serving a patron base made up primarily of new immigrants from Mexico with no books in Spanish

These are all examples of disconnects between selectors and the populations they serve. This is a pitfall that all selectors need to be recognize, and about which they should be periodically reminded. The exercise in the sidebar is a good starting point.

In general, as long as the materials you select meet the criteria laid out in your collection development policy, and you have logical reasons for requesting them, you probably won't go too far wrong.

Selection Exercise

Rank each of the following titles by how interested you are in using them and how important adding them would be to your library.

TITLE	ME	LIBRARY
New York Times		
People		
50 Shades of Grey (e-book)		
50 Shades of Grey (HBK)		
Complete Mother Goose		
#1 NYT Non-Fiction Best Seller		
The Hunger Games		
Downton Abbey Season 3 (DVD)		
Beatles White Album		
The Bible (Large Print)		

How similarly are the two columns scored? Why did you score them differently?

STEP 3: Determine the Budget

Although building the materials budget is usually the responsibility of the acquisitions unit, it can be the responsibility of selectors to track the budget to make sure there is enough money to pay for their selections. The ease or difficulty of this depends on how your library handles its budget. Tracking

the budget requires a high level of give-and-take between collection development staff and acquisitions staff. If you have access to multiple budgets, you
will need to indicate on each order the particular budget you want to use.
(Budgeting is discussed in depth in chapter 4).

STEP 4: *Make the Request*

Now that you have decided on the items you want to purchase for your
library, you need to communicate this to the acquisitions unit. This is done
via a request. Depending on the system your library uses, requests can take
any number of forms, ranging from small scraps of paper to computer-based
shopping carts. In general, requests should include information identifying
the item, which area of the library it is being bought for, which budget will
pay for its purchase, and who is requesting it.

IDENTIFYING THE ITEM

There are a variety of ways to identify an item you would like the acquisitions unit to order. To allow for cross-checking the title in the catalog and
current order file, most requests include the following.

ISBN (International Standard Book Number) is a ten- or thirteen-digit
code that identifies the country of origin, publisher, and title. ISBNs
are typically available only for books, although some DVDs have
ISBNs as well. Even though ISBNs are supposed to be unique, typos
do happen, and there are even some publishers that use the same
ISBN for multiple editions of a book. Therefore, ISBN alone is not
enough to uniquely identify a title.

Author/title (or *author and title*) seems like a simple unit of information,
but unfortunately it is not foolproof, thanks to situations such as
last-minute title changes by publishers or multiple editions or formats with the same title. In the case of audiovisual (AV) materials, you will see this information referred to as "producer/title" or
"director/title."

Publication or production information refers to the name and location
of the publisher and the year of publication. As more titles are

published in multiple countries and formats, the publisher's name is becoming more important to the identification process.

Format lets the acquisitions unit know which format to purchase. This is becoming more critical as more titles are being released simultaneously in multiple formats, for example, as a print book and as an e-book. Also, as publishers continue to consolidate, more formats may be released by the same publisher Examples of formats include hardback, trade paper, mass-market paper, large print, e-book, CD, e-Pub, Kindle, and the list goes on.

If you are requesting an item found through a vendor's website, ISBN, author/title, publication/production information, and format are usually provided. If you are requesting through another route, the publisher's website may still be useful for finding information; another good resource is a bibliographic utility such as OCLC's WorldCat.

The final information you need to provide with your request is an indication of the location of the item (i.e., where it is to be housed in the library), which part of the budget is paying for it, and any other notes that will let acquisitions, cataloging, and processing know of any special handling required.

Serials

Serials are materials that are purchased on an ongoing basis. They are ordered once and paid for annually, but are received part by part, over time. Serials include magazines, periodicals, standing orders (items, usually series, which are automatically ordered whenever a new volume is released), newsletters, and newspapers. The general term *serial* can include databases and aggregators, but since the process to select those is different from the materials listed above, they will be dealt with separately.

For many libraries, serials involve a multiple-year commitment, because of the need to maintain historical issues (backfiles) for reference and research purposes. Therefore, it is better not to add a title unless you are sure your patrons are going to need it and your library can afford to pay for it for several years. Whenever you are forced to cancel a serial, whether due to lack of budget, inflation, lack of use, or some other reason, there will be repercussions among your patrons.

As with monographs, there are four basic steps to selecting a new serial: identifying the publishing universe, choosing the items to request, budgeting for the items, and, finally, requesting them. Even though they are the same steps used when selecting monographs, there are some details that are different when you are selecting serials.

STEP 1: *Identify the Publication Universe*

Unlike monographs, which have several different options for identifying the publishing universe, the options for serials are much more limited. Usually there is a much smaller number of publishers and titles to choose from, which helps narrow the number of possible titles to evaluate. Four types of tools are used to determine the publication universe for serials titles: periodical directories, vendor catalogs, patron input, and retail stores.

Periodical directories are physical volumes or electronic databases that include information about the various serial titles available. They can be general directories such as *Ulrich's Periodical Directory* or its online equivalent, UlrichsWeb (ulrichsweb.com), or they can be focused quite narrowly, such as the Modern Language Association's *Directory of Periodicals.*

Serial vendors can help a library's serials workflow to run smoothly. As an intermediary between the library and periodical publishers, the vendor can manage subscription start dates, track price and title changes, negotiate international mail, and provide several other useful services. Most library business offices are not able to handle the amount of billing work required to run a separate account for each serial title. Vendors can aggregate serials billing, which allows you to make only a few payments to the vendor each year, as opposed to making many separate payments to each periodical's publisher. In addition, serial vendors will claim missing issues on your behalf, so you don't have to work directly with the publisher of each title. Finally, working with a serial vendor gives you access to its entire catalog of titles, and a directory of the titles offered by publishers with whom they have a relationship.

Patron input can be critical for choosing a serial title. Quite often when a patron requests a periodical, she requests a specific title, rather than a publication about a particular subject. This may be a great title to consider ordering because you already know you have some demand for it. If you are receiving requests for multiple titles in the same subject area, this list of titles gives you a starting place for deciding which you will select.

Retail stores can be a wonderful resource when you are starting a new collection. Go to local newsstands and see what they have on offer. Also ask them what sells best. Retailers will not invest space in titles that don't sell—they can't afford to, any more than a library can afford to pay for materials that are not being used. Some titles may be wildly inappropriate, but at least some of them will be good candidates for your collection. This can be especially helpful for titles in unfamiliar subject areas.

STEP 2: Select the Items to Request

How you choose between two equivalent serial titles can be fairly difficult—or it can be really easy. If you have a patron requesting a particular title, the choice is fairly easy. If you work in a school or academic library where there is need for more coverage of a particular subject, it can be more difficult to choose. When considering multiple titles, check sources like *Ulrich's* or the *Standard Periodical Directory* for reviews. Your vendor's website may also offer reviews. You can also request sample issues from the publisher or your serials vendor to see what the serial looks like, and use that information in your decision-making process.

One interesting tool available to you is a bibliographic utility, such as OCLC's WorldCat, which will show the number of member libraries that receive a title. This is not a perfect gauge of popularity, but it can give you a good idea. (This method works better for academic serials than for popular ones.)

In the end, as with all selection decisions, you will need to rely on your own judgment.

STEP 3: Determine the Budget

Budgeting for serials can get a little tricky because they represent a multiple-year commitment. One thing that many people outside the library—and even some inside—don't realize is that the cost of periodicals goes up every year, so if your budget does not increase from year to year, you will need to cut somewhere else to maintain all your subscriptions. Planning for these increases every year and adjusting subscriptions to fit the available budget is one of the worst parts of the acquisition librarian's job. It is always frustrating for staff and patrons to have a title cut because the library can no longer afford to pay for it. Before selecting a serial for purchase, you need to consider not only the current price of a subscription, but what its future price trend will be. This information is often available from your periodicals vendor, or even from the publisher.

STEP 4: Make the Request

Just as with requests for monographs, when sending a serials request to the acquisitions unit, you need to include several pieces of information. These serve to identify the title, give the publication information, and determine its location.

IDENTIFYING THE TITLE

There are a variety of ways to identify an item you would like to request. In order to cross-check the requested title in multiple places to ensure the accuracy of the information provided, most requests should include the following.

- The *ISSN* (International Standard Serial Number) is an eight-digit code that identifies the country of origin, publisher, and title. ISSNs are only available for serials, just as ISBNs are only available for books. Serials in all formats have ISSNs. ISSNs are supposed to be unique, but typos and other inaccuracies can happen. Therefore, ISSN alone is occasionally not enough to identify a serial.

- The *title* of a serial is also needed. Because publishers sometimes change the titles of their serials, finding a serial by title isn't always straightforward. For example, a title may change from *The Journal of Insignificant Matters* to *The Journal for Insignificant Matters.* Another complication is that different serials can have the same title. For example, there are hundreds of different serials with the title *Bulletin.*

- *Publication information* includes the name and location of the publisher, format, and the frequency with which the serial is published. As more titles are produced in multiple countries and formats, the publisher's name becomes increasingly important to the identification process.

Format lets the acquisitions unit know which format you want to purchase. This is becoming more critical as more serials titles are available in different bundles, which may print only, print and online, or online only.

Means of delivery should also be included. There is usually an additional charge if you want to receive a serial via first-class mail as opposed to library rate. If you are subscribed to titles published in other countries, it can get even more complicated. If you are requesting through a vendor website, the information about the means of delivery is usually provided. If you aren't, the information is usually available through the publisher's website.

Although most libraries shelve all their serials in one place, providing *location* information for your request is still critical. In public libraries, there is a choice between Adult, Young Adult (YA), and Juvenile collections, while in school and academic libraries, the location may vary by subject (e.g., Math, Geology, Social Studies, or other areas of the curriculum). Certain types of serials, for example, standing orders or annuals, may be located in the general collection.

Integrating Resources

In the world of libraries, integrating resources include several types of resources. They fall generally into three different groups. Online aggregators are services that provide online access to the digital full-text content of periodicals published by different publishers; databases are large regularly updated files of digitized information related to a specific subject or field; and indexes are alphabetically arranged lists of headings consisting of the personal names, places, and subjects treated within a published work or works. Although these three types of products all serve different purposes, they are usually grouped together as integrating resources because they all fall under this mode of issuance (see chapter 5) for collection development and acquisitions.

First, like serials, they are all subscribed to for a set period of time. The subscription is often referred to as a *license*, and it sets the length of the subscription. For those databases and indexes that offer perpetual archival rights, you still usually must pay an annual fee to maintain access.

Second, the library does not receive any physical copies of these materials. They are all in digital formats that are maintained on servers that belong to the vendor; you are paying for access. Once you order an item and the license is signed, someone from your library will manage the access (usually from either the acquisitions or systems department).

Third, many libraries acquire these products through memberships in consortia (associations of individual libraries or library systems). Although consortia can act as "buying clubs" for digital content, they also serve as a first level of review for materials you are evaluating for inclusion in your collection.

A fourth similarity is an outgrowth of the digital nature of these products. Unlike monographs and the majority of print serials, you can ask for trial subscriptions to online aggregators, databases, and indexes, as well as other integrating resources. Doing this is critical for evaluating user interfaces, ease of use, and a host of other issues that will go into your decision-making process.

STEP 1: Identify the Publication Universe

As is the case with serials, there is a much smaller pool of materials produced in these areas than with monographs. This is especially true for periodical and e-book aggregators. Thanks to these limited numbers, it is fairly easy to determine what products will meet the needs of your library.

Additional resources include any consortia that your library is a member of. As mentioned above, many consortia act as buying clubs, bringing several institutions together to negotiate better prices and service from various vendors and providers. Another way of finding out what's available is to talk to your peer institutions regarding what products they have subscribed to.

STEP 2: Select the Items to Request

There are several places to check for reviews of various integrating resources, online aggregators, databases, and indexes. Since many of these online services regularly update, upgrade, and change their services, make sure the review addresses the most recent version of the product. Reviews are available from standard review sources such as *Choice*, *Booklist*, or *Library Journal*. You can also find other libraries who already subscribe to services you are interested in and ask them for recommendations. This is even easier if you are working with a consortium, because you will already have a group of users to contact.

This is the point where requesting a trial subscription is critical. When you have identified the integrated resources you are interested in, contact their sales representatives and ask for trials. These usually run for thirty days, although some vendors will let them run for entire semesters for academic and school customers. You will usually need to provide some basic information, which is why acquisitions or Electronic Resources Management System (ERMS) staff will usually do the legwork to get them set up.

Don't forget to use some sort of evaluation system for each product you are getting a trial for. This will give you a basis to compare various products while allowing you to develop valuable feedback for the representatives with whom you are working. Evaluations can include online surveys you have developed to collect feedback, usage statistics from the vendor, and additional information provided by your library's reference and research staff.

STEP 3: Determine the Budget

Like serials, integrating resources, online aggregators, databases, and indexes represent an ongoing expense from year to year. Therefore, they must be budgeted with that in mind. Also, like every other type of material, the price will go up every year. An advantage is that there is more negotiation room for both the vendors and the library. Luckily for those doing collection development, most of this negotiation occurs in acquisitions.

STEP 4: Make the Request

Because the acquisitions unit has been active during the selection process for these resources through setting up trials, negotiating proposals with vendors, and so forth, by the time collection development formally requests an online aggregator, databases, or indexes database, selectors and acquisitions staff know what it is. However, there should still be a formal request, which will be the last opportunity to review the decision.

Once the request is placed, responsibility for the title moves to the next step in the process, acquisitions, which will be addressed in chapter 4.

Trends and Issues in Collection Development

There are several issues and trends that bear watching in collection development. These include:

Exclusivity among content providers and aggregators. Some publishers are making full text available only through certain aggregators. As the practice expands this will become a more critical area to track when evaluating aggregators, databases, and indexes.

"Just in time" rather than "just in case" collection development. At one time libraries tried to collect everything that they thought would ever be needed in our collections. As prices have gone up, budgets have gone down, and space has become tighter, more libraries are developing their collections on the "just in time" model. These models include such practices as Patron Driven Acquisitions, slip-based approval programs, and higher levels of rush ordering.

Importance of access over ownership. The concept that the amount of information a library can *access* through its various services is more important than the information it actually *owns* has become increasingly important over the years. Because of the explosion in publishing and online access in the past few decades, no library can hope to own all the content it needs. For example, although a library may only subscribe to 100 periodicals, it can access the content of another 12,000 titles through its aggregator subscriptions.

Open access. Open access is the practice of making content available over the Internet through other than subscription business models. Models currently at use for open access include publication charges, subsidies, and alternate subscription models. Open access also represents a change in copyright of academic publications away from traditional models to ones that allow the materials freely built on. This trend has been growing in recent years for several reasons. First, it has been in response to major serial publishers raising prices at the same time that library resources have been decreasing. This is a new model of scholarly communication designed to address the near monopoly some publishers have on major publishing in some fields. A second reason is to address problems of inequality of access to information from restricting access to institutions that can afford to purchase/subscribe to them. A third reason is to address the growing feeling that government-sponsored research should be freely available and not hidden behind the subscriptions and pay walls of various publishers.

Resources

Anderson, Rick. "Collections 2021: The Future of the Library Collection Is Not a Collection." *Serials* 24, no. 3 (2011): 211–215.

Mangrum, Suzanne, and Mary Ellen Pozzebon. "Use of Collection Development Policies in Electronic Resource Management." *Collection Building* 31, no. 3 (2012): 108–114.

Morrisey, Locke J. "Ethical Issues in Collection Development." *Journal of Library Administration* 47, no. 3/4 (2008): 163–171.

Pickett, Carmelita, Jane Stephens, Rusty Kimball, Diana Ramirez, Joel Thornton, and Nancy Burford. "Revisiting an Abandoned Practice: The Death and Resurrection of Collection Development Policies." *Collection Management* 36, no. 3 (2011): 165–181.

Tucker, Cory. "Collection Development: Current Options and Future Concerns." *Against the Grain* 19, no. 3 (2007): 44–50.

Acquisitions

The acquisitions unit is responsible for obtaining those materials selected by the collection development staff. Unfortunately, for most libraries this process is much more complex than running to your local bookstore or logging on to Amazon. It involves justifying, allocating, and tracking budgets; locating the items; determining pricing; encumbering funds; actually ordering and receiving the items; claiming them or cancelling them if they do not come in; handing them on to cataloging; and expending the funds. Other core functions of acquisitions include adding on-order records to your ILS, as well as confirming and maintaining access to electronic and online resources.

This chapter will cover:

- Budgeting
- Library materials vendors
- Monographs
- Serials
- Electronic integrating resources
- Trends and issues in acquisitions

Before You Begin

In the workflow of the technical services department, the acquisitions unit comes fairly early, because the materials must be ordered and received before any of the rest of the department's work except for collection development.

This unit is responsible for budgeting, ordering, and receiving all materials owned or accessed by the library. In many cases, it is also responsible for developing the lists from which the selectors choose.

Specialized Terms

Here are some of the specialized terms that you need to know before you start doing acquisitions work. Because acquisitions is one of those units that can combine functions from both internal business and public service parts of the library, many of these terms are from the business office.

Allocation—The part of the budget available for a specific use.

AV—A shorthand term for audiovisual materials.

Budget—The amount of money available for use by a person or organization. In this chapter the budget is the money available for the purchase or subscription to materials needed by the library.

Budget formula—A mathematical formula used to allocate available funds into specific areas.

Claiming—The process of notifying a vendor that ordered materials have not been received and replacements are needed.

Discounts—The difference between the list price of an item and how much the library actually pays for it.

Encumber/encumbrances—Money allocated to orders already placed but not yet received.

Fill rate—The ratio between the number of items ordered compared to the number of items received. This is usually expressed as a percentage.

Library materials vendors—Vendors that handle materials from multiple publishers.

Order confirmation—Notification from the vendor that an order has been received.

Packing slip—A list of materials that are packed in a single box or shipment.

Purchase orders—Formal notification to your business office that
   you have ordered something from a vendor.

Tracking—The ability to follow where an order is in the workflow of
   the library or vendor. Also used for locating an order once it is
   shipped.

Value-added services—Services, usually provided by the vendor,
   that add value to the product you are buying. In technical services, this can include a range of services from placing security
   strips to providing full cataloging and labeling services.

Vendor—A company with which the library does business.

Budgeting

Although the level of acquisitions staff's responsibility for the library's materials budget varies, they are usually given an amount by the library administration and are responsible for allocating, expending, and tracking that
amount. Creating materials budgets involves two processes: first, negotiating
the materials budget as part of the library's entire budget, and second, allocating the materials budget to various needs.

Negotiating the Materials Budget

Determining the materials budget as part of the library's whole budget is a
negotiation process between the head of the library and the library's funding
agency. As the person responsible for the materials budget, you need to be
ready to support the head of the library with various types of information.
This information can include the following:

Current and previous years' materials budgets. This information is needed
   to determine pricing and inflation trends

A list of which formats are actively collected. Because many funding agencies, politicians, and patrons still believe that the library only collects books, it is critical that these groups understand that libraries
   are not just warehouses of dusty books, but provide access to materials in multiple formats, with multiple pricing models.

The levels at which materials are actively collected. Materials costs vary
   according to the depth and breadth of the collections the library

is trying to maintain. Special and academic research library collections are probably the most expensive. However, even in school libraries, you will need to make your funding agency aware of the age, academic, and interest levels of the collections your library is trying to maintain.

Current budget allocations for different formats and levels. This is important both as a planning tool and as information critical to justify continuing and expanding funding for library materials.

Price trends for various formats and levels. Many library funders and users don't realize that libraries must pay for materials. If they do realize it, they may still not understand that the prices of library materials go up every year.

Information on new formats that may be added to the collection. In the past, when a new format was developed, an old format would disappear (e.g., the shift from vinyl records to cassette tapes to music CDs). However, in the rapidly changing technology environment of today, new formats are being added while older formats are still viable and in demand. An example of this would be adding downloadable books and e-books to the collection without being allowed to stop buying, or even cut back on, the number of hardcopy books ordered. This results in the materials-budget pie getting cut into smaller and smaller pieces.

Special circumstances that will affect the materials budget. These can be positive, for example, having to finance an opening-day collection or a major collection expansion. They can also be negative, as when the state cuts all library funding to balance the budget. These special needs can play havoc if you do not start planning for them as early in the process as possible.

Possible effects of various changes to the materials budget. In many cases there will be a series of budget exercises in which the library will participate. These can be questions such as, "What would you do if you had 10 percent more or 10 percent less money?" or "What would be the effect of outsourcing all selection?" You must be able to discuss these types of questions in a calm, rational manner that makes sense to your funding agency.

Documentation of how efficiently and effectively the materials budget is being spent. In many cases this is needed to convince your funding agency that it is better for the library to spend its budget itself rather than via a general purchasing department. Involving non-library purchasing units can be, and often is, an exercise in futility. For example, the authors had one very earnest purchasing agent explain to us that we could not pay for materials and services until after they have been received. Therefore, we could not subscribe to any periodicals.

In addition, you need to be ready to support the head of the library at various budget meetings, or even to represent the library by yourself. If you are called on to speak before a group about the budget, there are two critical things to remember. The first is to answer only the question being asked—if more information is needed, more questions will be asked. The second is to be honest—if you don't know an answer, say so and give a time when you will have the answer. Making answers up on the fly can and will get you into more trouble in the future than not having an answer ready.

If you are at a meeting in support of the head of your library, remember to keep your facial expression neutral at all times, and to offer comments only when asked. Believe it or not, a poorly timed arched eyebrow can change the entire tone of a discussion.

This discussion has barely scratched the surface of how technical services fits in to the budget as a whole. For more information, a good resource is *Fundamentals of Technical Services Management,* cited in the list of resources at the end of this chapter.

Allocating the Materials Budget

The second process in building a materials budget is allocating the materials budget to specific levels and formats of materials. This is an involved, complicated process that generally requires the following steps.

STEP 1: ONGOING COSTS

Determine the amount needed to cover ongoing costs for the next year plus any additions your institution wants to make. These include serial subscriptions, database and electronic access fees, and other materials for which there are annual fees. These costs can be negotiated with the vendor, although for planning purposes there are sources that can provide guidance about how prices are expected to change in the coming year. Several resources for this type of information are given in the in the list of resources at the end of the chapter.

STEP 2: ONE-TIME COSTS

Determine the amount needed to maintain levels of purchasing in one-time cost areas, plus any additions your institution wishes to make. These include books, DVDs, compact disks, and other types of materials. Again, in many cases pricing for these materials can be affected by your negotiations with each vendor. For planning purposes, articles addressing price trends are given in the list of resources at the end of this chapter. Very often, one of your best resources for this type of information is the vendors with whom you are working. Most of them are glad to provide pricing forecasts.

STEP 3: CARRYOVER

Determine how much over or under you will finish up the current year's budget. The importance of this step depends on how your funding institution handles its budgets from one fiscal year to the next. The two most common variations are:

Continuous funding. This occurs when any budgeted funds you have left at the end of the fiscal year get moved forward into your new budget, or, if you have overspent your budget, the funds to cover the overspending are subtracted from your new budget at the beginning of the next fiscal year. This is a double-edged sword, because if you do not spend all your budgeted funds your funding agency may get the impression that you don't need as much money as they've been giving you. On the other hand, overspending your budget reflects badly on your ability to manage funds on behalf of the library. So you need to be very careful when walking this tightrope to expend your entire budget without going over.

Single-year funding. This occurs when your budget is opened at the beginning of the fiscal year and closed at the end of the fiscal year.

Unspent funds are returned to the general fund and overspending is covered from other sources. Note that if you overspend, you may be reprimanded. This is one of those areas where you need to work with your business manager to stay out of trouble.

STEP 4: NEW BUDGET

Find out the total amount your funding agency has budgeted for materials for the next planning period. This was discussed above in "Negotiating the Materials Budget."

STEP 5: COMPARE

Compare the total of Steps 1 through 3 with the amount in Step 4.

STEP 6: INCREASE/DECREASE

If the allocated budget (Step 4) exceeds the total of your projected costs (Steps 1 through 3), congratulations! You can allocate more money to areas that need it. If your projected costs (Steps 1 through 3) are greater than your allocated budget (Step 4), you will need to either find more money somewhere, cut your ongoing expenses, cut your one-time expenses, or all three.

As simple as these steps sound, the mechanics of developing a budget are complicated. Each funding agency will have different rules and priorities that influence budget development. As an agent of the library, you will need to adjust your budgeting methodology to meet those priorities.

Budget Allocation Methods

Once the overall materials budget is finalized, it can be subdivided to whatever level of detail needed in order to track it. This can be very broad level, for example, monographs and serials, or it can be at a very detailed level, for example, adult mysteries for a particular branch. How you set up your fund structure should be as detailed as you need it to be without imposing too much confusion on the system. A very helpful resource for this is the format of the previous year's budget.

Unfortunately, there are no hard and fast rules about how to allocate your materials budget across the different programs you need to support. There are several different methodologies that can be used. A few of them are detailed below along with some advantages and disadvantages of each.

All the examples that follow are based on the statistics for a fictional library shown in tables 4.1 and 4.2.

TABLE 4.1

Collection statistics

		NUMBER OF ITEMS	PERCENTAGE OF TOTAL COLLECTION
Collection		100,000	100%
Total adult		75,000	75%
	Nonfiction	40,000	
	Fiction	30,000	
	Audiobooks	500	
	Music and DVDs	4,500	
Total Juvenile		25,000	25%
	Nonfiction	12,500	
	Fiction	7,500	
	Audiobooks	100	
	Music and DVDs	1,000	
	Picture Books	3,750	
	Kits	150	
Formats (Adult and Juvenile)			
	Books	96,250	95.8%
	Music and DVDs	5,500	0.5%
	Audiobooks	600	2%
	Magazines (titles)	75	0.075%
	Kits	150	0.175%

TABLE 4.2
Circulation statistics

CIRCULATION		400,000	
	Adult	180,000	45%
	Juvenile	220,000	55%
Library Cards		100,000	
	Adult	45,000	45%
	Juvenile	55,000	55%
Price Index	Total	100	
	Adult	75	
	Juvenile	25	

HISTORICALLY BASED BUDGETING

The most common methodology for budget allocations is historical practice. This involves looking at how the budget was allocated in the past and continuing it into the future. Assuming no change to the total budget, there would be no changes to the allocations. This is shown in table 4.3.

Unfortunately, this is rarely the case. Serials have price increases every year, so you usually can't simply superimpose a budget from one year onto the next. Using the same assumptions as before, but adding an expected 5 percent inflationary increase to periodical pricing. This would look like table 4.4.

TABLE 4.3
Flat budget

FUND LINE	CURRENT FISCAL YEAR	UPCOMING FISCAL YEAR
Adult	150,000	150,000
Juvenile	50,000	50,000
Periodicals	5,000	5,000

TABLE 4.4

Flat budget with 5 percent increase to periodicals

FUND LINE	CURRENT FISCAL YEAR	UPCOMING FISCAL YEAR
Adult	150,000	149,875
Juvenile	50,000	49,875
Periodicals	5,000	5,250

TABLE 4.5

Flat budget with detailed allocations

FUND LINE	CURRENT FISCAL YEAR	UPCOMING FISCAL YEAR
Adult	150,000	149,875
Nonfiction	90,000	89,938
Fiction	40,000	39,937
Music and DVDs	20,000	20,000
Juvenile	50,000	49,875
Nonfiction	12,500	12,469
Fiction	17,500	17,469
Music and DVDs	7,500	7,469
Picture Books	12,500	12,469
Periodicals	5,000	5,250
Adult	3,500	3,625
Juvenile	1,500	1,625

TABLE 4.6

Formula based on circulation

FUND LINE	CURRENT FISCAL YEAR	CIRCULATION. PERCENTAGE	UPCOMING FISCAL YEAR
Adult	150,000	45%	90,000
Juvenile	50,000	55%	110,000

Note that in this case the increase in periodicals was funded by small cuts in the adult and juvenile budgets. This always must balance.

To take it to the next step, let's see what it looks like when some additional allocation lines are added, as shown in table 4.5.

The total budget is the same, but the amount allocated to each area changes. In this case, periodicals are being protected while all other areas are being cut. Note that if you follow this type of budget adjustment for too many cycles, the periodicals will begin taking over the entire budget and squeezing out other materials. Ideally, your funding agency will at least cover inflation of periodical prices with an increase each year. However, if this doesn't happen—or doesn't happen on a regular basis—you will need to cut periodicals at some point. Ways of doing this are discussed in chapter 3.

FORMULA-BASED BUDGETING

Formula-based budgeting uses one or more variables to determine how to allocate the materials budget. Determining which variables to use is up to each library. The only criterion is that they be easily measureable and consistent across the collection. Who must agree to the formula can vary by library. Agreement may need to come from the acquisitions unit and the business office, or it may need to include all the selectors and even members of the library board. Even the number of variables used can vary quite a bit between libraries. We've found that three is a good number (at least to start with), because with more than three, it's possible to spend more time collecting data than buying materials. Fewer than three is almost a waste of time.

Any type of variable can be used when developing a formula. Examples include circulation, number of card holders, demographics, reserves placed, price index, collection size, and collection age. In general, anything that can be measured and is relevant can be used as a variable.

Three common variables, which our examples will be built around, are average price, number of items circulated, and the numbers of adult versus juvenile cardholders. All three are fairly easy to find either in reports in the library industry or through information you have in your ILS circulation system.

Continuing with our examples from above, let's look at some sample formula-based budgets as seen in table 4.6.

TABLE 4.7

Formula based on circulation and average price

FUND LINE	CURRENT FISCAL YEAR	CIRCULATION. PERCENTAGE	AVERAGE PRICE	UPCOMING FISCAL YEAR
Adult	150,000	45%	24.00	120,000
Juvenile	50,000	55%	8.00	80,000

Note that in this example, periodicals aren't included in the formula because it is assumed that they do not circulate. If they do circulate, the budget for them would be included in the rest of the budget and split out later in the process. By using only circulation, you can see that the result would be a fairly major realignment of the budget from adult materials to juvenile materials. Unfortunately, adult materials tend to cost more than juvenile materials, so that must be taken into account. This is shown in table 4.7.

In this case, the assumption is that on average an adult book costs three times what a juvenile book does. When you compare this to the previous example, you can see that although the juvenile budget does get some additional money based on circulation, it does not gut the adult budget, which has a higher cost per volume.

Another variable that can affect collection usage is the number of each type of patron. This example adds a third variable that reflects this by including the number of adult library cards versus the number of juvenile library cards. This is shown in table 4.8.

As you can see, the large number of juvenile cards will once again swing the formula back towards higher funding for juvenile materials.

Budget formulas can be as simple or as complicated as you wish. As stated previously, the authors have found that more than three variables generally become unwieldy, resulting in more time spent developing the formula than the amount of money involved merits.

HYBRID-BASED BUDGETING

A third methodology is a hybrid of the methods just discussed. One hybrid that is particularly useful is to divide the budget into parts setting aside one amount to be allocated based on historical or minimal funding levels with

TABLE 4.8

Formula based on circulation, average price, and library card holders

FUND LINE	CURRENT FISCAL YEAR	CIRCULATION, PERCENTAGE	AVERAGE PRICE	NUMBER OF CARDS	UPCOMING FISCAL YEAR
Adult	150,000	45%	24.00	60,000	102,000
Juvenile	50,000	55%	8.00	120,000	98,000

TABLE 4.9

Hybrid-formula budgeting

FUND LINE	CURRENT FISCAL YEAR	MINIMUM	CIRCULATION, PERCENTAGE	AVERAGE PRICE	FORMULA FUNDS	TOTAL UPCOMING FISCAL YEAR
Adult	150,000	75,000	45%	24.00	60,000	135,000
Juvenile	50,000	25,000	55%	8.00	40,000	65,000

the rest of the budget being allocated based on some type of formula, as seen in table 4.9. This is just one example of the many possible hybrid methods.

NON-ALLOCATION-BASED BUDGETING

A fourth method is to use no methodology at all. Materials are purchased as they are requested, regardless of where or how they fit in the collection. This method is not recommended, because it can lead to both workflow and collection development issues as the fiscal year progresses. Nonetheless, it is a methodology that is used by a number of small—and even not so small—libraries.

Expending

Now that you have built the budget, by whatever method you used, what do you do with it? First you need to set up a ledger. A ledger is a list of allocations, with space to record what is being paid from each allocation. This can be done in the ILS if it includes an acquisitions module, or built it in a basic

TABLE 4.10

Sample ledger

DATE	DESCRIPTION	AMOUNT ENCUMBERED	AMOUNT PAID	TOTAL	RUNNING TOTAL
01/01/12	Opening Balance				15,000
01/02/12	January Book Order	250	175	425	14,575
02/02/12	February Book Order	300	32	332	14,243
03/02/12	March Book Order	500	0	500	13,743
03/03/12	Special Order	0	75	75	13,668

spreadsheet program. This can even be done by hand in a ledger similar to a check register, which can be as detailed as necessary. Regardless of what you choose to use as a ledger, you'll find this is another one of those areas where making friends with the business manager of your library can be very helpful. Some funding agencies have particular reporting requirements that need to be addressed when developing your ledger. The exact requirements of your ledger will also vary by what kind of budget system your library uses. In general, the analogy to the check book register works well. Table 4.10 is a sample ledger.

A ledger is a critical tool for tracking how you are expending your money. In this example, you are given all the necessary information about when an order was placed, what was ordered, what the retail price was, what the final price was, what the total for the order was, and how much you have left in that particular allocation. The definitions of the data elements are:

Date—When the transaction was added to the ledger (in this example, it is the order date).

Description—The details of the transaction. Each of these lines might have a layer beneath it that shows the transaction details to the title level.

Amount encumbered—This is a critical and very confusing concept. Most libraries get some kind of discount on the materials they order through various contracts and agreements. However, many libraries are required to encumber the list (full) price for an item when they order it. When an item is ordered, it is necessary to place a reserve on, or encumber, enough money to pay for the full price of the item, even if a discount is expected. The cost of any value-added services that are being provided by the vendor should also be added. The encumbered price of an item would be:

list price + value-added services + shipping and handling = encumbered price

Amount paid—This is the amount actually paid for an item. It is usually:

list price – discount + value-added services + shipping and handling = amount paid

Because the amount paid is usually less than the amount encumbered, all the materials on an order may be received and paid for, and money will still be encumbered by that order. This is recaptured and spent on something else.

Total—The remaining encumbrance plus the amount actually paid.

Running total—The amount still left to encumber or spend in this allocation.

The good news is that if you are using the acquisitions module of an ILS, much of this accounting is done for you. But it is still critical to understand what goes on in the background. There are libraries that have had money taken away from them at the end of the year because they didn't recapture and spend their over-encumbrances.

Library Materials Vendors

Library material vendors, which handle materials from multiple publishers, can be your best friends or your worst nightmares. When working with any vendors, it is very important to talk to your business office to determine the rules that govern your interactions. Even something as harmless as letting a vendor representative, or rep, take you to lunch can violate the rules governing interactions with vendors.

Libraries may use several materials vendors, or none at all, depending on the requirements of their funding agencies. They can have direct contracts or work through state or consortial contracts. Contracts can be very general—"We will spend our entire book budget with you"—or very narrow—"You will be our first choice for juvenile, animated movies in both Blu-ray and DVD formats." There are materials vendors specializing in periodicals, books, audiovisual materials, foreign language materials, databases, Mexican foto-novelas, and more.

Before you decide whether or not to use materials vendors, find out what your library has done before, talk to library administration, and contact the purchasing unit for your funding agency to find out what regulations may apply. There are, of course, advantages and disadvantages to contracting with various vendors for materials.

Advantages include:

- guaranteed and predictable discounts
- better discounts and prices on value-added services
- predetermined shipping and handling costs
- fewer questions about where to send a particular order
- benchmarks for establishing and evaluating service levels
- clearly defined expectations
- pre-established grievance procedures

Disadvantages include:

- substantial up-front investment of staff resources to develop, evaluate, and award bids
- loss of flexibility when placing orders
- ongoing investment of staff resources to monitor contract compliance
- limited ability to take advantage of publisher's specials

In light of these concerns, contracting with a vendor is a major step that shouldn't be undertaken without forethought and preparation. If you decide to do so, work with the library's business officer and your funding agency's purchasing office to develop the needed request for proposal, evaluation criteria, and finally the contract award.

Care and Feeding of Vendors

Vendors and vendor reps can be your best allies, rock-solid partners, or your worst enemies. Here are ten things to remember when working with them.

1. Vendors are in business to make money. That is how they survive, so be reasonable.
2. Don't take problems with vendors out on their reps. Most will do what they can to fix issues if you work with them.
3. Smile! If you are having a bad day when your rep comes to call, let her know, and don't take it out on her. She is just doing her job.
4. Communicate with vendors. If you are having issues with them, such as problems with customer service, or billing, or are expecting budget cuts, the sooner you tell your vendors, the better.
5. If there is a problem, discuss it calmly and rationally, and give examples. People seldom go out of the way to help a raving monster.
6. Don't make promises you can't keep. Even salaried reps depend on their commissions, and they may be counting on your orders.
7. Make time for your reps. The time you invest in these relationships will pay off in the long run.
8. If a rep comes in for a scheduled meeting, make sure you are there. On the other hand, if a rep shows up without an appointment, don't feel bad about making him cool his heels for a few hours.
9. Make sure your rep is included in any communication with her home office. Otherwise, she may not be aware of what the home office has told you, which leads to confusion and misunderstandings.
10. Don't play favorites. The rep you snub today may be the only one who has critical product information tomorrow.

Monographs

Monographs are those materials you only pay for once. These include books, DVDs, CDs, and the like. At the most basic level, there are four steps to monographic acquisitions: verification, ordering, adding the title to the ILS, and receiving. These are shown in figure 4.1.

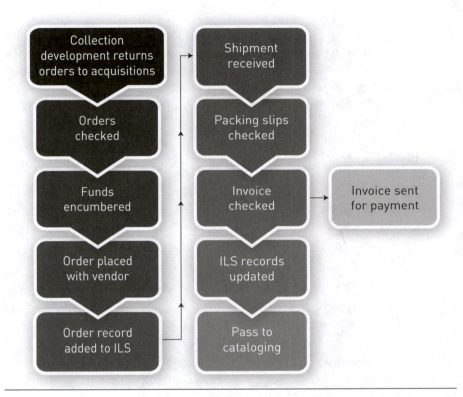

FIGURE 4.1

Basic workflow—acquisitions—monographs

STEP 1: *Verification*

This is the process of confirming the details of the resource you want to order in the vendor's system. Verification can be fairly easy if you have all the information you need and it is accurate. It can also be difficult if all you have is partial or inaccurate information. The key is finding the correct match points, which are the data elements that confirm you have located the correct item. These are usually author, title, ISBN, date of publication, publisher, and edition statement. Remember, the more points that match, the greater the chance that you have found the correct item. If you can't find an item that matches all the required data points, contact the person requesting the item with the best information you can find, and let him confirm whether what you've found what he wants.

There are several sources of acceptable data to base your orders on. These include vendor catalogs and websites, OCLC's WorldCat (www.worldcat.org), and the Library of Congress's online catalog (www.catalog.loc.gov). Alternative sources to confirm order information are online booksellers such as Amazon (www.amazon.com) or Barnes & Noble (www.barnesandnoble.com). The mechanics of order verification will vary by how much information is provided with the order. In general, you will want to rank your search from the most unique piece of information to the least unique.

Search by International Standard Bibliographic Number (ISBN) (if available). This number is unique to each item, but is generally only available for books.

Search by the author/title. This is generally unique information, but if multiple editions or formats are available, a search will find all of them, and you will need to determine the correct one for your order. In the case of AV materials, you may need to search by the director/title; producer/title; or performer/title.

Search by title. Searching by title can be effective for relatively unique titles. For example, *The Curious Case of the Dog in the Nighttime* will return a small number of records. However, a search for a not-very-unique title may bring up more results than you can sort. For example, a search for the title *The Great War* on Amazon brings up more than 200,000 results. However, a title search is often the best way to find audiovisual materials.

If you are unable to find a match for the item, ask the person who selected it for more information. In many cases, if you can find out where she heard about the title, you can track it back for additional information. If it is a self-published title, you will probably need to contact the author directly; this is becoming increasingly common because more people are publishing on their own.

STEP 2: Ordering

This is the step where you select the vendor or retailer you wish to use. You will also need to attach all needed accounting data. Finally, the order must go to the appropriate vendor.

Select the vendor. This will vary depending on your vendor contracts, type of material being ordered, and publisher. If you have a variety of vendors you can use, you should have guidelines for deciding which vendor to use.

Add fund accounting data to the order. This includes vendor account, budget/fund line being encumbered, purchase order number, and other information needed for tracking the materials budget. Work with your library's business officer to determine how much information you need to include.

Transmit the order to the vendor. This will also vary by the vendor you are using. Today orders are often transmitted via the Internet or EDI. However, phone, fax, e-mail, and even letters are still used on occasion,

After you transmit the order to the vendor, you will usually receive some type of confirmation, which may include an order status that will indicate if the item you have ordered is available, backordered, or out of print. See the section on order statuses below for more information.

STEP 3: Adding Titles to the ILS

If your library is using the acquisitions module of your ILS, you will need to add the materials you ordered to it. If your library does not use the acquisitions module, you will need to develop some way of tracking your orders to avoid unintended duplication, which will also be helpful for tracking the status of orders you have outstanding with various vendors.

The information you will need to add to the acquisitions module was determined during the order verification process. It is usually a brief bibliographic record that includes author, title, publisher, and publication date, as well as the accounting information. In many cases, these records will be available from your vendor, which will send them as part of the order verification process. In this case you will only need to upload them to your system's catalog. At the worst, you will need to manually input them. Work with your cataloging staff to determine which information you need to include in the brief bibliographic record.

STEP 4: Receiving

Now that you have verified and ordered your materials, they will begin to arrive from your vendor. This leads to the final step in the acquisitions process: receiving. Receiving is the process of checking the materials to make sure they are what you ordered and are in good condition, updating their status in the acquisitions module, and approving the related invoice for payment.

Review the packing slip. Every shipment should have a packing slip or a form that shows what should be in the shipment you have received. The first thing you need to do is unpack all boxes and find the packing slip. While you are unpacking the shipment, check materials for damage that may have occurred in binding or shipping. If damaged materials are found, contact your vendor's customer service for instructions.

Make sure everything that should be there is there. If it is, continue processing the materials received.

- If it isn't, make sure that you have all the boxes related to that shipment.

- If you have all the boxes, contact your vendor's customer service department before going any further. It is much easier to handle any issues as soon as they come up and the shipment is still all in one place.

- If you don't have all the boxes, contact your vendor's customer service representative and ask him to trace the shipment from its end.

- If there are materials in the shipment that do not appear on the packing slip, call your vendor's customer service department to determine what to do with them.

Update the order record. Whether you use your ILS's acquisitions module or an independent order tracking system, you need to update it to reflect the receipt of the ordered materials.

- Locate the record in your order system.

- Update required fields (e.g., date received, unit price, shipping and handling, and so forth).

- Update other information, if available.

At this point the materials are ready to send to the next step in the process. This will usually be cataloging, which will be discussed in chapter 5.

Order Statuses

Throughout the order process you may receive order status reports from your vendor. These include:

Available—The item is in the warehouse and there is enough stock on hand to fill your order.

Backordered—The item is still in print, but there aren't enough copies in the warehouse to fill your order. The vendor has ordered more copies, and will fill your order when the additional copies come in.

Out of stock—The vendor doesn't have enough to full your order, and when they tried to get more, the publisher was out too. The publisher may or may not make more copies.

Out of print—The publisher has declared that they will not be publishing any more copies and the vendor doesn't have enough to fill your order.

Shipped—The vendor has pulled the item and sent it to you.

Cancelled—The vendor has cancelled your order. This will usually include an explanation.

Many vendors have real-time inventory information available on their websites. This should be monitored during the order process to avoid encumbering the budget for materials that aren't available.

Serials

Serials are those materials that are either received in parts over time, like magazines, or are paid for on a regular basis, like annuals and standing orders. Although these two types of materials are handled separately in cataloging, in acquisitions they are handled together and referred to collectively as serials.

At the most basic level, there are four steps to the acquisitions process for serials, as shown in figure 4.2. These are verification, ordering, adding to the ILS, and check in/receiving. Unlike monographs, it is not generally necessary to add a record to your ILS when you order a new serial title. ILS records, if added at all, will be created by cataloging after the subscription has been confirmed.

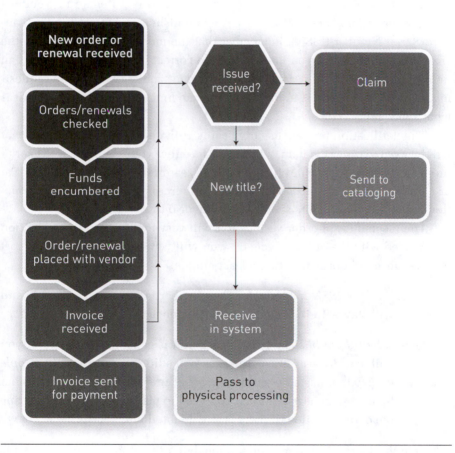

FIGURE 4.2
Basic workflow—acquisitions—serials

STEP 1: *Verification*

Verification is the process of confirming the details of what you want to order and confirming that it exists. It is fairly straightforward if you have all the information you need, and the information is accurate. However, the process can become difficult if you have information that is incomplete or inaccurate. This can be even more complicated for serials, because publishers sometimes make small changes to the title unexpectedly. The key is finding the correct match points to confirm that you've located the correct items in a vendor's system. For serials, these are usually title, publisher, and International Standard Serial Number (ISSN). Remember that the more points that match, the greater the chance that you have found the correct item. If you can't find an item that matches all the data points provided, contact the person requesting the item with the best information you can find, and let her decide if it is what she wants.

The verification process usually begins with checking in the system that will be used to order the item, which may be either your vendor's or the serial publisher's. If you can't find the item there, search sources such as WorldCat or *Ulrich's Periodical Directory*. Alternative sources to confirm order information are online booksellers such as Amazon or Barnes & Noble.

The mechanics of order verification will vary by how much information is provided with the order. In general, you will want to search from the most unique piece of information to the least unique.

Search by the ISSN if available. This number is unique to each title and will stay with it through most title changes.

Search by title/publisher. This information is generally unique, but you will need to be aware of differences in editions. For example, *People en Espanol* has a US edition, a Mexican edition, and several other Spanish-language editions. You need to make sure you are ordering the correct edition. If there is any doubt, double-check.

Search by title. A title may be unique, but a search may bring up a large number of identical titles in a variety of formats.

Search by format. Many, if not most, titles are now available in both print and electronic editions. Make sure you've ordered the format you want and that you have identified the correct version of the title.

If you are unable to find a title that matches the request, go back to the person who requested it and ask for more information. In many cases if you can find out where he heard about the title, you can track it back for additional information. Note that publications from organizations can be very difficult to find if you don't have the full name of the organization.

STEP 2: Ordering

This is the step where you select the vendor or retailer you wish to use. Remember to attach all required fund accounting data. Finally, the order must be sent to the appropriate vendor.

- *Select the vendor.* This will vary depending on vendor contracts, type of materials being ordered, and the source of material being ordered. If you have a choice of vendors, you should create guidelines for deciding which vendor to use. When working with serials, it is much easier to work with one or two primary materials vendors whenever possible rather than directly with the publisher.

- *Add fund accounting data to the order.* This includes vendor account, budget/fund line being encumbered, purchase order number, and any other information needed for tracking the materials budget. Work with your library's business officer to determine how much information you need to include.

- *Transmit the order to the vendor.* The process will vary according to the vendor you are using. Today, orders are generally transmitted via the Internet. However, phone, fax, e-mail, and even letters are still used on occasion, depending on vendor and library requirements. After you transmit the order to the vendor, you will usually receive some type of confirmation.

STEP 3: Adding Titles to the ILS

If your library is using the serials module of your ILS, you will need to add the titles you ordered to both the acquisitions and serials modules. If your library is not using the serials module, you still need to add ordered titles to your acquisitions system. You will also need to develop a method to track when issues are received or—more importantly—not received, so you can claim them. Historically, this was done using a physical file where each serial title had a card with all the information on the title. It was not uncommon for serials not to be added to the ILS at all. But with advances in ILS technology, serials modules have gotten more efficient, and many libraries have moved their serials management online. The process of adding a serial to your ILS involves two parts. The first is the bibliographic record, which is usually handled by the cataloging unit. The second is the check-in record, which includes information on how often you expect to receive a title; this should be added before you first receive a title. This critical information lets you know when you have missed an issue and need to claim it. Work with your cataloging unit to determine which information should be recorded and who will do so.

STEP 4: Receiving

Now that you have verified and ordered your materials, you will begin to receive invoices for them. This will usually include information about the start and end dates of the subscription, how it will be mailed to you (first class, third class, or media rate), and, in the case of electronic subscriptions, how to access the title online. Use this information to work with the cataloging unit and the person handling your ERMS to make sure all the information needed for your catalog and for accessing the content is available. Unlike print monographs, you won't receive large shipments of materials with a packing slip. These materials will come in at regularly scheduled times such as weekly, monthly, quarterly, annually or irregularly depending on the publication schedule of the publisher. Note that in some libraries, serial check-in is a public services function. It is included here because it is, in fact, part of the acquisitions process.

> *Compare the item in hand to the check-in record.* You will probably receive at least a few serial issues every day, which you will need to check in manually or in the ILS. When checking in a title, you should look at several things. These include:
>
> - Title (to confirm that the publisher hasn't changed it unexpectedly)
> - Volume and issue number
> - Date (to make sure you didn't miss an issue)
> - Damaged or lost parts

Update the check-in record. Whether you use your ILS's serials module or an independent serials system, you must update it to reflect the receipt of the issue in hand.

- Add the date, volume number, and issue number of the item in hand.
- Add the date it was received.
- Update any other available information.

At this point the materials are ready to send to the next step in the process. This will usually be physical processing.

However, if after a few weeks you notice you have not received some issues of a serial, or some issues have arrived in damaged condition, you will need to claim those issues. This involves notifying your vendor or publisher that you need a replacement for one or more issues of a serial. The process will vary by vendor or publisher. Some companies have very liberal claiming policies, but others are very strict or won't provide any back issues at all. The time limit to claim a missing issue can vary from a few days or be open-ended. It is a good idea to check once a week, or at least once a month, to determine if any issues weren't received. If you are using your ILS serials module, this can be as easy as running a report. If you are using a manual system, it will require looking at every card to see what has or hasn't arrived.

Electronic Integrating Resources

Electronic integrating resources are online or digital resources in which some parts change from time to time, while the resource as a whole remains essentially the same. They include databases, aggregator indexes, and other subscription-based online materials that are not updated frequently, but do change in minor ways over time.

At the most basic level, there are four steps to acquiring electronic integrating resources. These are verification, ordering, licensing, and accessing. Because access to electronic resources often becomes available soon after ordering, it is less common for acquisitions records to be used for these materials. If these materials are represented in your catalog, the records will be added by cataloging staff after access has been confirmed.

Before you begin the order process, check with the resource's producer to see if you can set up a trial subscription for your institution. These are usually thirty to ninety days long, and give you the opportunity to explore the resource and see if it will do everything you need it to. During the trial you can evaluate search functions, data coverage, accessibility, and a number of other areas that can help you confirm if you want to pay for access to this particular product. If you do have a trial, the verification process will take place at that point.

STEP 1: Verification

Verification is the process of verifying the details of what you want to order and confirming that it exists. This is a fairly easy process if you have all the information you need and it is accurate. It can become complicated if all you have is inaccurate or incomplete information. A URL is usually included when you request electronic resources, so verification is generally simple. You should to be careful to verify levels of access. The difference between citation-only access and full-text access is huge in terms of both amount of content available and cost. Make sure you confirm what level your institution wants.

STEP 2: Ordering

This is the step where you select the vendor or retailer you wish to use. Because electronic integrating resources are generally available from a single source, this is seldom a difficult decision. Usually you will only need to research whether or not the desired resource is available through a consortium your institution is a member of. You will still need to have all the ledger information. If the resource can be IP authenticated, you will need to provide the IP ranges for your institution.

STEP 3: Licensing

Licensing is where electronic resources become very different from monographs and serials. In the current business model, libraries do not buy electronic integrating resources, but instead license them. When you order one, you receive a legally binding license. To protect yourself, your library, and your funding agency, licenses should be reviewed very carefully. In many cases the library cannot be the legal signatory, so be sure to contact your institution's business office and your funding agency's purchasing office to determine what rules govern licensing for your library.

There are some key issues that should be addressed in the license:

- How much is your institution being charged?
- What is the method of authentication—IP, unique user names and passwords, or shared user name and password?
- Will the resource be available at multiple sites?
- Can the library provide remote access, and if so, under what terms?
- Can materials be used for interlibrary loan, and if so, under what terms?
- How many users can access the resource at the same time?
- Are there any download restrictions, and if so, what are they?

Remember that the license is a legal document that describes what you will be able to access, how you will access it, how the access is limited, and for how long the access will be available. It is critical that you review it carefully. Don't be afraid to ask questions or request clarifications. Like any legal document, a license may go back and forth a few times before everyone signs off on it. Make sure to update the effective dates of the license if the negotiation period goes on too long.

STEP 4: Accessing

After the license is signed by both parties, you will receive instructions on how to access your new resource. This will usually include the information to include in your ERMS, URLs to opening pages, and in many cases, the appropriate bibliographic records for adding the resource to your ILS. This final step is making sure the ERMS is updated, sending the records to cataloging so they can add the resource to the catalog (if appropriate), and testing to make sure you have the access you are supposed to before making it available to your patrons.

Trends and Issues in Acquisitions

Acquisitions units are experiencing many of the same changes as other areas of libraries. Issues and trends impact all types of libraries. Although details may differ (especially in those areas involving technology), the broad issues and trends are fairly consistent. These larger trends can be broken down into technology, expectations, and resources.

Technology

No one disputes that technology is changing rapidly. What is less clear is how changing technology affects library acquisitions. The biggest change is in the formats of the materials being acquired. There was a time when libraries collected print books, print magazines, vinyl LPs, and—if you were lucky—35 mm filmstrips. Today, the average small library generally must collect:

- print books in hardback, trade paper, and mass market paper
- audiobooks
- downloadable books in print and audio
- print serials
- electronic serials
- music CDs
- DVDs (and in some cases Blu-ray)
- databases

As technology continues to evolve and new formats emerge, what the library collects to satisfy the needs of its patrons will also change. This leads to the second major trend: expectations.

Expectations

As technology has increased awareness of and access to materials, patrons' expectations have also increased; they believe that the library should be able to acquire everything anyone wants, immediately and in unlimited supply. More library staff time is required to managing these expectations and educate library patrons, staff, and funding agencies.

Even though accessing all this material is becoming more seamless, the behind-the-scenes work that goes into providing this seemingly simple access is becoming increasingly complicated. Since this work happens out of public view, most library patrons and funding agencies (and even many library staff) don't even realize that it goes on, let alone the amount of resources invested in it.

Resources

As with all parts of the library, acquisitions is faced with having to do more with less. Materials budgets have been trending downward for several years, while cost inflation of library materials has simultaneously been trending upward. This results in de facto budget cuts, even when the materials budget remains static.

The number of staff resources devoted to acquisitions has also been shrinking. To an extent, this has been offset by increases in efficiency, but if the trend continues more libraries will have to outsource most of their acquisitions functions.

Final Thoughts

Acquisitions is a major unit in most libraries. The materials budget is usually the largest budget outside of personnel, acquisitions is responsible for its expenditure. But beyond monitoring how the budget is expended, acquisitions is responsible for making sure it is expended efficiently and effectively to support the library's goals and objectives. Although this is a major task, it is only an early step in the process of making materials available for the library's patrons. Once an item is received, it moves on to cataloging, which will be discussed in chapter 5.

Resources

Fischer, Karen S., Michael Wright, Kathleen Clatanoff, Hope Barton, and Edward Shreeves. "Give 'Em What They Want: A One-Year Study of Unmediated Patron-Driven Acquisition of e-Books." *College & Research Libraries* 73, no. 5 (2012): 469–492.

Intner, Sheila, with Peggy Johnson. *Fundamentals of Technical Services Management*. Chicago: American Library Association, 2008.

Johnson, Peggy. *Fundamentals of Collection Development and Management*. Chicago: American Library Association, 2014.

Koehn, Shona L., and Suliman Hawamdeh. "The Acquisition and Management of Electronic Resources: Can Use Justify Cost?" *Library Quarterly* 80, no. 2 (2010): 161–174.

Kubilius, Ramune K. "Issues in Book and Serial Acquisition: 'Something's Gotta Give!'" *Against the Grain* 24, no. 2 (2012): 60–63.

Pomerantz, Sarah B. "The Role of the Acquisitions Librarian in Electronic Resources Management." *Journal of Electronic Resources Librarianship* 22, no. 1/2 (2010): 40–48.

Urbano, Cristóbal, Yin Zhang, Kay Downey, and Thomas Klingler. "Library Catalog Log Analysis in E-Book Patron-Driven Acquisitions (PDA): A Case Study." *College & Research Libraries* 76, no. 4 (2015): 412–426.

Von Hielmcrone, Harald. "The Digital Library and the Law—Legal Issues Regarding the Acquisition, Preservation and Dissemination of Digital Cultural Heritage." *Microform & Digitization Review* 41, no. 3/4 (2012): 159–170.

5

Cataloging

At its most basic, cataloging is the process of adding records to a library's catalog. Each record in the catalog stands in for a resource the library owns or has access to. The record must describe the resource in enough detail that a library user can tell it apart from similar resources, as well as figure out if it is a resource they want. The record must also provide ways for users to find it when they search the catalog, and it must tell them how the item it represents can be accessed. Like any other library service, cataloging should always focus on the needs of library users.

Cataloging is a complex process that follows multiple rules and standards, and therefore may seem a little daunting. However, just as you don't need to know how to replace a spark plug in order to drive a car, you don't need to know how to create a MARC 347 field in order to catalog. You simply need to know some basic principles and consistently apply them.

There are different cataloging workflows for physical resources and online resources. Physical materials are sent to cataloging after they are received in the acquisitions area. As shown in figure 5.1, once they are cataloged, they are sent on for physical processing, and from there are shelved and made available for patrons to use. Online materials are cataloged shortly after electronic access to the materials has been established, and are available for patrons to use as soon as the catalog record is created (see figure 5.2).

This chapter will cover:

- The catalog
- Shared cataloging

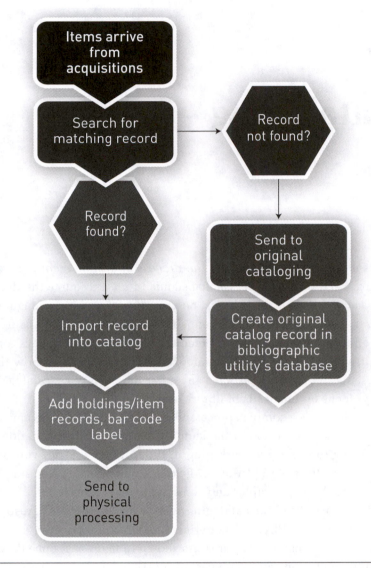

FIGURE 5.1

Basic workflow—cataloging—physical materials

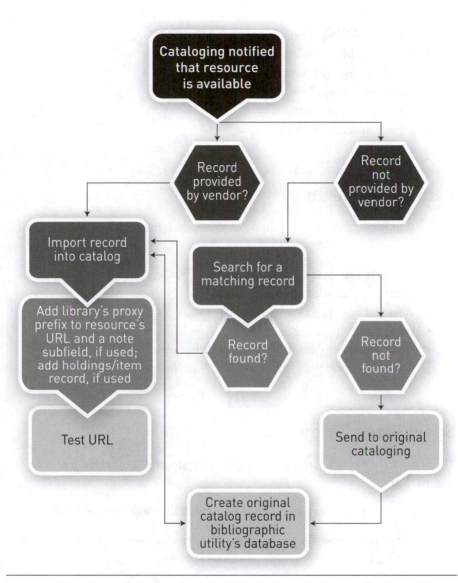

FIGURE 5.2

Basic workflow—cataloging—electronic materials

- Copy cataloging versus original cataloging
- Bibliographic utilities
- Local cataloging practices
- Copy cataloging
- Outsourced cataloging
- Trends and issues in cataloging

Before You Begin

Before you begin cataloging, you must determine the answers to these questions:

- What content standard is used at your library?
- What classification system is used?
- What set of subject terms is used?
- What ILS is in place?
- What bibliographic utility does your library use?
- What local practices are in place at your library?

Specialized Terms

There are many specialized terms used in cataloging. These are just a few of them:

Access point—A searchable unit of information in a catalog record.

Bibliographic record—An entry in a library catalog that describes and provides subject access to a resource.

Bibliographic utility—An organization that maintains a huge database of bibliographic records that participating libraries contribute and copy.

Call number—A code, often unique, assigned to a library resource by a cataloger. A call number usually consists of a subject classification code, one or more Cutter numbers, and a date.

Classification system—A system of numeric or alphanumeric codes for arranging library materials by subject.

Content standard—A set of guidelines for describing resources and creating access points.

Copy cataloging—Copying (and perhaps editing) a bibliographic record that already exists.

Copy holdings record—A record linked to a bibliographic record that contains information about where a resource is located, its copy number, and (for multipart resources) which parts the library owns.

Cutter number—A code made up of letter(s) and numbers, added to a call number to help maintain alphabetical order.

Edition—All copies of a resource that have the exact same content, format, and publisher.

Integrating resource—A resource in which new content is integrated into the whole, leaving the resource somewhat changed but essentially the same.

Internet Protocol (IP) address—The unique address of a particular computer.

Item record—A record linked to a bibliographic or holdings record that represents one unit (e.g., one volume) of a resource. An item record may include a bar code, a copy number, item type, and location.

Mode of issuance—The way in which a resource is issued. A resource may be issued monographically, serially, as an integrating resource, or as part of a series.

Monograph—A resource that is complete in itself, either in one part or a defined number of parts.

Online Public Access Catalog (OPAC)—The side of a library's catalog that is visible to, and searchable by the public.

Original cataloging—The process of creating a new record for a resource from scratch (as opposed to copy cataloging).

Outsourcing—Contracting with a vendor to provide a service to a library. Authority control and cataloging are the most common technical services activities that are outsourced.

Program for Cooperative Cataloging (PCC)—An international organization of libraries that work together to create original catalog records in a timely manner.

Proxy server—A computer server that acts as an intermediary between a patron seeking an electronic resource and the resource itself. Its purpose is to limit the use of certain licensed electronic resources to patrons who have borrowing privileges. Each patron is authenticated by logging in with identifying information and password.

Serial—A resource issued in discrete parts over time, with no predetermined end, and usually bearing numbers or dates or both.

Series—a group of related materials, each with its own title as well as a series title, published by the same publisher, and often bearing a series number.

Shared cataloging—The practice of sharing catalog records among libraries, made possible by shared cataloging standards and bibliographic utilities.

Standard digital format—An agreed-upon digital framework that gives catalog records a structure, and allows them to be displayed and transmitted by computers.

Subject heading—A subject term, chosen from a list of preferred subject terms, that is added to a bibliographic record to provide subject access.

Uniform Resource Locator (URL)—An Internet address.

The Catalog

A library's catalog is a collection of records that represents the holdings of the library, that is, what the library owns or has access to. The catalog organizes library materials in a way that is logical, allows patrons to search for and find materials they want, and lets library staff know what the library has in its collections. It may also track statistics about library materials. Library catalogs have a "front side" and a "back side." Figures 5.3 and 5.4 illustrate how the front side and back side of the catalog look. The front side is what library patrons see: the online public access catalog (OPAC). The back side is the cataloging module of the library's ILS, where catalogers do their work.

Mastering the art of French cooking

Title:	Mastering the art of French cooking / by Julia Child, Louisette Bertholle and Simone Beck.
Author:	Child, Julia.
Other Author(s):	Bertholle, Louisette.
	Beck, Simone.
Publisher:	New York : Knopf, 1961.
Description:	Book club ed.
	726 p. : ill. ; 24 cm.
Format:	Book
Subjects:	Cooking, French.
Notes:	A Borzoi book.
	Includes index.
Location:	Branson Library
Call Number:	TX719 .B388 1961b Copy 1
Number of Items:	1
Status:	Available

FIGURE 5.3

Record viewed in the "front side" of the catalog

000			00686cam a2200241|a 4500
001			306828
005			20121206092141.0
008			871129s1961 nyu 001 0 eng d
035			‡a ocm12294282
040			‡a TAP ‡c TAP ‡d WaOLN
049			‡a IRUU
090			‡a TX719 ‡b .B388 1961b
100	1		‡a Child, Julia.
245	1	0	‡a Mastering the art of French cooking / ‡c by Julia Child, Louisette Bertholle and Simone Beck.
250			‡a Book club ed.
260			‡a New York : ‡b Knopf, ‡c 1961.
300			‡a 726 p. : ‡b ill. ; ‡c 24 cm.
500			‡a A Borzoi book.
500			‡a Includes index.
650		0	‡a Cooking, French.
700	1		Bertholle, Louisette.
700	1		Beck, Simone.

FIGURE 5.4
Record viewed in the "back side" of the catalog

The back side of the catalog is made up of bibliographic records and two or three other kinds of records: *authority records, copy holdings records,* and sometimes (depending on the ILS), *item records.* (Authority records will be discussed in chapter 7.) Bibliographic, copy holdings, and item records (if present) are linked to each other in a hierarchical structure, as seen in figure 5.5. The bibliographical record is at the top of the hierarchy, one or more copy holdings records are at the next lower level, followed by (if present) one or more item records for each copy holdings record.

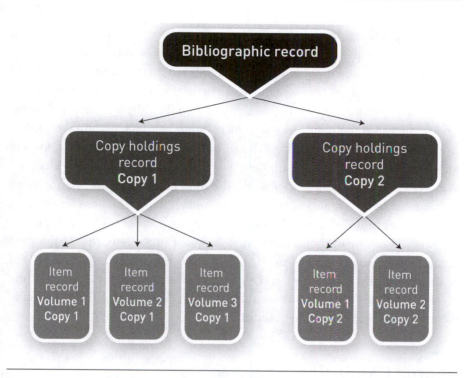

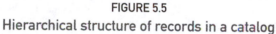

FIGURE 5.5

Hierarchical structure of records in a catalog

A bibliographic record includes *descriptive cataloging information* (i.e., author, title, publishing information, and physical description) and *subject information* (subject classification number and subject headings). A useful way to think of a bibliographic record is that it describes any copy of a particular resource. For example, the same bibliographic record could be used to describe any copy of the 2007 Houghton Mifflin edition of the print book *The Singing Life of Birds*, by Donald Kroodsma, whether it held by the British Library or the Seattle Public Library.

Both physical and electronic resources need *copy holdings records*. Copy holdings records are important because they give a detailed picture of what the library owns: where a resource is shelved (for physical resources); how many copies of a resource the library has; and, in the case of multipart resources (such a serial with many different issues), which parts of a resource the library holds. For example, a copy holdings record for the second copy of the book *The Singing Life of Birds* in the Beloit Public Library's catalog would give its location (Adult Non-Fiction), its call number (528.1594 Kroodsma), and its copy number (copy 2). If a library has multiple copies of the same resource, each copy has its own copy holdings record. No matter how many copies/holdings records there are, each one links to the same bibliographic record.

An *item record* represents one physical item held by a library. Its record usually includes the item's location; its call number; its copy number; information about whether it can be checked out, and for how long; and a unique identifier, usually a bar code number. For the Beloit Public Library's copy 2 of the book *The Singing Life of Birds*, the item record includes its location, call number, copy number, and bar code number. It also includes a code that indicates that the book may be checked out for three weeks at a time. An item record may also include information about how many pieces the item contains. For example, *The Singing Life of Birds* has an accompanying CD of birdsongs, so it would have a piece count of two: one for the book, and one for the CD. If a library's ILS does not have item records, item information is recorded in the copy holdings record.

Shared Cataloging

Because most library materials are mass-produced, every copy of a resource, no matter which library it is in, is virtually identical. It wouldn't make sense for catalogers at every library to create an individual catalog record from scratch for each library's copy of a publication. To make cataloging more efficient, catalogers have developed and adopted uniform cataloging rules and standards over the years. Because of these rules and standards, catalogers describe and provide access to resources the same way, so that catalogers at different libraries can share records with each other. There are four basic kinds of rules and standards used by catalogers:

1. *Content standards* provide guidelines for describing resources and creating certain access points (specific pieces of information, including author and title, which can be searched in the catalog). The title of a book and the name of its author are just two of many possible access points in a record. For more information about content standards, see appendix A.

2. *Classification systems*, such as Dewey Decimal Classification (DDC) and Library of Congress Classification (LCC), provide

detailed codes to represent various topics, and allow resources with similar topics to be located close together. For more information about classification systems, see appendix B.

3. *Subject term lists*, such as *Sears Subject Headings*, are lists of preferred subject terms. Catalogers select terms from the list to include in bibliographic records for materials on those subjects. For more information about subject term lists, see appendix C.

4. *Standard digital formats*, such as Machine-Readable Cataloging (MARC), provide standard ways of organizing the bits of data that make up an electronic catalog record. For more information about MARC, see appendix D.

Copy Cataloging versus Original Cataloging

Most cataloging done in libraries is *copy cataloging*, a process that involves downloading a record from a bibliographic utility and adding it to the local catalog. When a resource arrives in the cataloging area, a cataloger searches a bibliographic utility's database for a record that matches the resource. If a matching record is found, it is imported into the local catalog. If no matching record is found, the resource requires original cataloging. Some libraries set aside materials that require original cataloging for a set amount of time, then search again for a record. Many times another library will have created a record by the time the second search is conducted. This practice is especially useful for resources in foreign languages, in unusual formats, or any resource for which your staff lacks the required expertise. Copy cataloging is preferred whenever possible, because it is much more efficient than original cataloging. The vast majority of library materials have records available from a bibliographic utility and only need copy cataloging.

Original cataloging, that is, creating a record from scratch, is much more difficult and time-consuming than copy cataloging, and should only be done if no alternative is available. Most original catalogers learn to catalog by working with an experienced cataloger over an extended period of time, much like an apprenticeship. Because there are so many codes and standards at play in a given catalog record, there are hundreds of ways to make a mistake. Having an experienced cataloger check a novice's work is extremely helpful, and learning from mistakes is an important part of the process. In addition, cataloging is not always cut-and-dried. Often, an original cataloger must choose among a few possible ways of describing a resource, so she must develop a good sense of "cataloger's judgment," that is, reasoning out solutions based on cataloging principles. Interestingly, not all original catalogers will arrive at the same solution for the same problem. Here again, guidance from an experienced cataloger is invaluable. Because original cataloging is so difficult to learn, it is beyond the scope of this book.

Bibliographic Utilities

A bibliographic utility is a massive database of catalog records. When a library subscribes to a bibliographic utility, it is entitled to contribute bibliographic records to the database (original cataloging) and download records from the database (copy cataloging). This means that if one library contributes a record, a cataloger at any other participating library may download that record and add it to his library's catalog. Participating libraries agree to follow certain sets of standards when contributing records to the utility's database. Bibliographic utilities are a crucial part of catalogers' ability to share records with each other.

The most familiar bibliographic utility is OCLC, founded in 1969 as the Ohio College Library Center. A newer utility, SkyRiver, was formed in 2009.

Local Cataloging Practices

Once the copy cataloging record is in the local catalog, it may be edited to fit a library's own way of doing things. The answers to the questions in "Before You Begin," above, are part of how your library does things, but there are probably other, more specific practices developed over time at your library. This collection of "how we do it here" information is called *local practices*. Although there are many kinds of local practices, only two will be discussed here: cataloging treatment and classification.

As outlined in chapter 3, every library resource has a mode of issuance, that is, the way it is published. There are four kinds of materials, based on mode of issuance.

1. *Monographs* are publications that are issued in one part or a predetermined number of parts. A monograph is usually represented by a single bibliographic record in the library catalog.

2. *Serials* are published in distinct parts that are issued over time, with each part having the same title, and no intended end date. All the issues of a serial are described on just one bibliographic record.

3. *Integrating resources*, like serials, are published over time, but instead of being made up of distinct parts, the resource stays basically the same although parts of it change. For cataloging purposes, an integrating resource is represented by just one record.

4. *Series* are collections of related monographs issued by the same publisher.

Monographs, serials, and integrating resources are each subject to their own special cataloging rules, so it is important to know to which of these categories a resource belongs. Fortunately, for the first three kinds of resources, the mode of issuance is usually easy to figure out. Series, on the other hand, can be a little tricky. It can be difficult to tell if a resource is a monograph or one issue of a serial. To make things even more complicated, some resources can be cataloged either way. For example, *The 2015 Old Farmer's Almanac* looks a lot like a monographic book, but because there is an *Old Farmer's Almanac* published every year, with the same title every time, it could also be cataloged as one issue of a serial. It is up to the individual cataloger to decide whether to catalog *The Old Farmer's Almanac* as a series of monographs or as a serial.

The choice of how to catalog an ambiguous resource is called *cataloging treatment.* No matter the cataloging treatment chosen, it is crucial to catalog things like it the same way every time, because library users (and staff!) could become confused if some issues of a serial are on the catalog record for the serial, and others are cataloged as stand-alone monographs. If you catalog the first book of a series as a monograph, you should make sure you catalog every book in the series the same way. If you catalog a series of maps as a serial, you should make sure you add every map to the serial record, and do not catalog any individual map on its own monographic record. One way to make sure you treat a resource the same way it was treated in the past is to search your library's catalog for the series title. It's best to search in multiple ways—as a serial title, as a series title, and using keywords from the title. If your search turns up a serial record, you will know that the series is being treated as a serial at your library. If your search returns a number of monographic records with the series title in each record, you will know that the series has been cataloged as a series of monographs at your library. If your search returns both a serial record and monographic records, you will need to investigate further.

Another common local practice is to classify certain materials by a system that deviates from the standard classification system in use at your library. This is usually done to make it easier for patrons to find materials. For example, DVDs may be organized by title instead of by call number. In this scheme, *Alice in Wonderland* would be shelved before *Bernie*, which would be shelved before *Cabaret.* Another example is classification of biographies. In DDC, biographies should be classed in various subdivisions of the number 920; however, many libraries have opted to simply use the classification 921 for every biography, followed by an alphabetical Cutter number for the subject of the biography. Under this system, a biography of Benjamin Franklin would have the call number 921 Fra.

There are many other kinds of local practices, including writing the call number on a resource in a certain place, shelving large-sized materials together in a special location, and adding a note to a record to recognize the donor of the resource. It's important to learn what your library's local practices are, especially when you are new at the job.

There are different ways to find out about local practices. First, look for documentation. Keep in mind that the documentation may be in print or electronic form, so look at both computer files and paper files. Second, ask colleagues (if you are the only cataloger at your library, there may be no one to ask). Finally, look in the catalog. A catalog search can tell you whether a particular resource has been cataloged as a series or a serial in the past, how biographies and DVDs are classed, and just about anything else you have a question about. However, when you look in the catalog for guidance, don't rely on just one example—look at several to make sure you see a pattern. You may very well find that things have not been handled consistently in the past. In those cases, you will need to decide how to proceed in the future and whether to change older records to match your decision. Be sure to document your decision—for yourself, your colleagues, and your successors.

If your library has documented local practices, wonderful! You have much less work to do; however, you will still need to make sure the documentation is complete and up-to-date. If there is no documentation, create it!

If you have more than one cataloger at your library, it's a good idea to keep the documentation in a single place that everyone can access—a shared drive on your library's computer network, a webpage, a wiki, a notebook that is always kept in the same place, or whatever works best for you. Keeping your documentation in electronic form makes it easier to edit and keep current.

While you are in the process of discovering, updating, or documenting local practices is a good time to evaluate those practices. Ask, "Why are we doing this?" If no one can remember, or the answer is, "We've always done it this way," take a hard look at that practice and decide if you really need to keep it. Sometimes a practice made sense in an earlier version of the library's catalog, or was instituted to address a problem that no longer exists. In these cases, the local practice should be modified or eliminated.

Copy Cataloging

Even though copy cataloging is less complex and time-consuming than original cataloging, there are still some important principles to keep in mind:

Make sure the record will fit with the other records in the catalog. Whenever a resource is cataloged, the record that represents it is added to the large group of records that make up a library's catalog. The records in the catalog are meant to make sense together, and much of what catalogers do is to ensure that the catalog works well as a whole. For example, adjusting call numbers to maintain alphabetical order helps maintain a useful arrangement of resources on the shelf or in the catalog.

Make sure there is only one bibliographic record for a given edition of a title. The same title may be published in different editions over time. Each edition is similar to the other editions, but is also different in ways that matter to library patrons. Each different edition should have its own bibliographic record, and all copies of the same edition should be represented by the same catalog record. This reduces confusion for library patrons and staff. It's a good idea to search your library's catalog before adding a new bibliographic record to ensure that there isn't an existing record for the edition of the resource you are cataloging.

Attention to detail is crucial for most technical services work, and cataloging is no exception. The resource being cataloged should always be closely examined and carefully compared to any record that seems to be a match for it.

Copy Cataloging Physical Materials: Step by Step

In this section you will find step-by-step instructions for copy cataloging materials that have a physical form. This category includes printed books, DVDs, music CDs, printed maps, kits—any resource that takes a physical form. A section on copy cataloging online electronic resources follows this one.

STEP 1: WHAT IS IT?

Because there are different cataloging rules and practices for different types of materials, the first step in cataloging a resource is figuring out what kind of resource it is. There are two important aspects of a resource to pay attention to: its mode of issuance and its type.

Mode of Issuance

As discussed in chapter 3 and earlier in this chapter, mode of issuance is the way a resource is published. A resource might be a monograph—something that stands alone and is complete in itself; a serial—a collection of parts issued over time where each part has the same title but different content and a different date or number; or an integrating resource—a resource that remains essentially the same, but has some parts that change over time. In addition, some monographs are issued as parts of a series. Here are some guidelines for figuring out how a resource was issued:

Is the resource complete in one part or in a predetermined number of parts, like a single DVD, or a book that is published in two volumes? If so, it is probably a monograph. The following are all monographs: a music CD by the Rolling Stones; a road map of Oregon; a copy of Harper Lee's book *To Kill a Mockingbird*.

If the resource is complete in one part, does it have a series title and (perhaps) a number, but still have its own unique title? If so, it is probably a monograph that is part of a series. An example of a monograph that is part of a series would be the book *Prince Caspian*, a book in the series The Chronicles of Narnia by C. S. Lewis.

Does the resource title include words like "journal," "newsletter," "bulletin," "annual," or "magazine"? Does it have numbering, for example, "Volume 2, number 6," and/or a date? Are there similar resources with the same title but different numbering and dates, and different content? If so, it is probably an issue of a serial. For example, the April 29, 2013, issue of *Sports Illustrated* is one issue of a serial.

Is the resource updated from time to time while remaining essentially the same? If so, it is probably an integrating resource. For example, the webpage of your local bank is updated from time to time, but since most of the information remains the same, it is considered an integrating resource. Another example of an integrating resource is *Affirmative Action Compliance Manual for Federal Contractors*, a resource that is issued as an updating printed looseleaf; that is, it is issued in a binder that is updated from time to time by adding new pages with updated content and removing pages with outdated content. Keep in mind that a resource with any content can be a monograph, serial, or integrating resource. DVDs are often monographs, maps may be issued as monographs or serials, and most webpages are either serials or integrating resources.

Type

Mode of issuance is just one aspect of a resource of concern to catalogers. Another aspect, the resource's type, is what the kind of resource it is. For example, a resource can be a printed book, a map, a DVD, an e-book, and so on. In this book, "type" is used as a catch-all term for attributes of a resource that RDA breaks out into three categories: *content type*, *medium type*, and *carrier type* (see appendix A for more information). AACR2 does not categorize resource types in this way. In most cases, a resource's type is apparent from its physical characteristics. For example, a book is usually a bound volume made up of pages with text on them. A DVD is usually in a special kind of case common to DVDs, with text that indicates its content is a movie issued as a DVD. A music CD is usually issued in a case with an insert that lists the performer(s) and tracks. You may need to use a machine of some kind in order to figure out the content of a resource. For example, an optical disc might contain music files, video files, or data files. Sometimes the only way to really know what kinds of files it contains is to put it into a player (probably a computer's disc drive) and access the files to see what they are.

STEP 2: HOW ARE RELATED RESOURCES HANDLED AT MY LIBRARY?

This step is important for a resource that appears to be part of a series or an issue of a serial. As discussed in the section on local practices, search the library's catalog by the series/serial title, including a keyword search using the words that make up the title. Follow the established practice at your library. If the item is an issue of a serial, simply add the issue to the existing serial record, and skip the rest of the steps in this section. If it is part of a series, continue as described below.

STEP 3: DOES IT ALREADY HAVE A RECORD IN MY LIBRARY'S CATALOG?

This step is especially important if you share a catalog with other libraries. A search by ISBN should suffice, although a title search is also recommended. If there is already a record in the catalog, skip to Step 8.

STEP 4: IS THERE A MATCHING RECORD OR RECORDS IN MY BIBLIOGRAPHIC UTILITY?

Once you've figured out what a resource is, how similar resources are handled at your library, and determined that the catalog doesn't already have a record for the resource, the next step is to find a MARC Bibliographic record that matches it in your library's bibliographic utility. Since a bibliographic utility may have more than one record that appears to match the resource you are cataloging, it is important to choose a record that is an exact match for the resource, and has the most accurate, complete information. This section presents match points for most kinds of library materials. You may find that a record doesn't include every possible match point, but the match points it does have must exactly match what is on the resource. If a match point is present in the record and does not match the resource, the record is not a match.

Match points for books

    ISBN (MARC field 020)

    Author (MARC fields 100, 245 $c)

    Title (MARC field 245)

    Edition (MARC field 250)

    Publisher (MARC field 260 or 264)

    Physical description (MARC fields 300, 336, 337, 338)

Match points for serials

    ISSN (MARC field 022)

    Title (MARC field 245)

    Dates (Fixed fields, MARC field 260 or 264)

    Publisher (MARC field 260 or 264)

    Frequency of publication (MARC fixed field Frequency)

    Physical description (MARC fields 300, 336, 337, 338)

Match points for audiobooks

    ISBN (MARC field 020)

    Author (MARC fields 100, 245)

    Title (MARC field 245)

    Edition (MARC field 250)

    Publisher (MARC field 260 or 264)

    Physical description (MARC fields 300, 336, 337, 338)

    Narrator (MARC field 511)

Match points for music recordings

    Performer (MARC field 100 or 110)

    Title (MARC field 130 or 245)

    Label (MARC field 260 or 264)

    Uniform Product Code (UPC) (MARC field 024)

    Catalog number (MARC field 028)

    Format (MARC fields 300, 336, 337, 338)

    Track list (MARC field 505)

Match points for video recordings

    Producer (MARC field 245 $c or 508)

    Director (MARC field 245 $c or 508)

Title (MARC field 130 or 245)

UPC (MARC field 024)

Cast (MARC field 511)

Distributor (MARC field 260 or 264)

Languages (MARC fields 041, 546)

Release date (MARC field 260 or 264)

Copyright date (MARC field 260 or 264)

STEP 5: WHICH RECORD IS BEST?

As mentioned above, a bibliographic utility will often have more than one matching record for the same resource. Which one is best? Here are some points to consider when choosing a record.

Are the classification system and subject headings vocabulary the same as those used at your library? For example, if your library uses DDC, you should prefer a record with a Dewey call number over a record with a LCC call number.

Is the content standard used to create the record the same one used at your library? If your library uses AACR2, you would prefer an AACR2 record over an RDA record, and vice-versa.

Is a foreign language used in the cataloging description? You should prefer a record in which the descriptive fields are in English.

Is one record more complete than another? A good indicator of completeness is the value in the MARC Encoding Level fixed field. Here are the most common values found in that field:

blank	Full-level, input by a PCC library
1	Full-level, material not examined
2	Less-than-full level, material not examined
3	Abbreviated level
4	Core level
5	Partial (preliminary) level
7	Minimal level
8	Prepublication level

If OCLC is your bibliographic utility, you will see a few other codes used in this field:

I	Full-level, input by OCLC participating library
K	Less-than-full level, input by OCLC participating library
L	Full-level, added through a batch process
M	Less-than-full level, added through a batch process

Full-level cataloging is the most desirable, whereas Core and Minimal levels are less desirable. A good look at the record will also give you an idea of how complete it is.

Other things to look for:

- The record should have a full call number and subject headings.
- All the information in the record should be accurate, but pay special attention to access points.

When cataloging a newly released publication, you may see a Cataloging-in-Publication (CIP) record. CIP records are input by the Library of Congress as part of a program to create bibliographic records for materials that are not yet published. If no more complete record is available, it is fine to use a CIP record; however, there are a couple of points to keep in mind. First, check all the information very carefully, especially the title and subtitle. Sometimes a resource's title changes between the time the CIP record is created and the time it is published. Second, be aware that you will probably need to add some information, especially page numbers, because typically this information wasn't available when the CIP record was created.

STEP 6: HOW DO I GET THE RECORD INTO MY CATALOG?

When you've found the best record that is an exact match, you need to bring it into your local ILS. This is done through software provided by your bibliographic utility and software in your ILS. Typically, you will export the record from your bibliographic utility, and then import it into your library's ILS. If your library's acquisitions department has already added a provisional bibliographic record for the resource, you will need to either replace that record or merge your record with it. How this is done depends on your ILS.

STEP 7: HOW SHOULD I EDIT THE RECORD? (OPTIONAL)

You may choose to edit the bibliographic record after you import it. Here are some typical ways catalogers edit bibliographic records:

- Adding page numbers and other information to CIP records.
- Changing the classification number to match local practices.
- Adjusting the Cutter number part of the call number to maintain alphabetical order.
- Adding notes that apply to the local copy, for example, "This book was donated by Esther L. Berquist."
- Changing entries for names, some titles, and subject terms to match their preferred forms. This is a form of authority work, and is discussed in more depth in chapter 7.
- Deleting certain MARC fields that are considered superfluous for local patrons. Examples of these are fields created for vendors to use, fields for use by national libraries in other countries, and subject headings in languages not used by your library's patrons.

STEP 8: WHAT OTHER RECORDS SHOULD I ADD?

Once the bibliographic record is in your ILS, you will create a copy holdings and, depending on your ILS, an item record for it. Copy holdings and item records give detailed information about what a library has in its collection, letting patrons know what a library has, and allowing library staff to keep track of the collection. The copy holdings record usually includes the call number, a copy number, and, for multipart resources, which parts the library owns. The item record, if present, usually includes a unique bar code for the resource, a copy number, and the number of pieces that make up the resource. If there is no item record, this information is recorded in the copy holdings record.

STEP 9: HOW SHOULD I MARK THE ITEM?

This step may be done as part of cataloging or as part of physical processing. A resource will usually be marked with a property stamp. In addition, the call number may be written somewhere on the resource. Sometimes security tags are also added in cataloging.

STEP 10: WHERE DOES THE RESOURCE GO FROM HERE?

This is the point where the resource leaves the cataloging area. Many libraries have separate physical processing units (see chapter 6 for more information on physical processing). Other libraries do physical processing as part of cataloging. Once the resource leaves physical processing, it goes to be shelved and is available for patrons to use.

Copy Cataloging Online Electronic Resources: Step by Step

Copy cataloging an online electronic resource is similar to copy cataloging a physical resource, but there are a couple of important differences. First, e-book vendors often provide MARC records free of charge along with access to their e-books. These records are usually provided in a file that is imported into the catalog using special procedures for importing multiple records at the same time. Second, because there is no physical processing involved, the workflow ends when cataloging is finished.

STEP 1: WAS A MARC RECORD PROVIDED WITH THE RESOURCE?

If yes, do a little checking to make sure the way the record complies with your local way of handling this kind of resource. For example, if you catalog a particular series of e-books as a serial, you wouldn't want to use a bibliographic record that catalogs one title in the series as a monograph. If, after checking, the vendor has supplied a record you can use, skip to Step 5.

If no, go on to Step 2.

STEP 2: WHAT IS ITS MODE OF ISSUANCE?

As discussed in chapter 3 and earlier in this chapter, mode of issuance is the way a resource is published. It might be a monograph—something that stands alone and is complete in itself; a serial—a collection of parts issued over time where each part has the same title but different content and a different date or number; or an integrating resource—a resource that remains essentially the same, but has some parts that change over time. In addition, a monograph may be issued as part of a series. Here are some guidelines for figuring out how an online electronic resource was issued:

Is the resource complete in one part or in a predetermined number of parts, like a single e-book?

If the resource is complete in one part, does it have a series title and (perhaps) a number, but still have its own unique title? If so, it is probably a monograph that is part of a series. An example of a monograph that is part of a series would be the book *Quality Control Applications*, a book in the series Springer Series in Reliability Engineering.

An electronic online serial will usually be identified as a serial when the acquisitions unit notifies you that the library now subscribes to it. You will want to check to see if your library also subscribes to the print version of the serial. Some libraries catalog both print and electronic versions of a serial on the same record. If your library does this, you will simply edit the print serial record to include both versions.

Is the resource updated from time to time although remaining essentially the same? If so, it is probably an integrating resource. For example, the webpage of your local bank is updated from time to time, but since most of the information it contains remains the same, it is considered an integrating resource. A database (a collection of related electronic data stored together in one or more files) may also be an integrating resource. An example of a database is *Birds of North America*, a database of information about birds maintained by the Cornell University Lab of Ornithology.

STEP 3: HOW ARE RELATED RESOURCES HANDLED AT MY LIBRARY?

This step is important for a resource that appears to be part of a series or an issue of a serial. As discussed in the section on local practices, search the library's catalog by the series/serial title, including a keyword search using words that make up the title. Follow the established practice at your library. If the item is an issue of a serial, simply add the issue to the existing serial record, and skip the rest of the steps in this section. If it is part of a series, continue on as described below.

STEP 4: DOES IT ALREADY HAVE A RECORD IN MY LIBRARY'S CATALOG?

Since the same e-book may be provided by different vendors, it's a good idea to do a search of the catalog to check if you already have a bibliographic record for a particular e-book. If there is already a record in the catalog with access from the same vendor as the e-book you are cataloging, check with the acquisitions unit to see if the e-book may have been ordered by mistake. If the access is provided by a different vendor, skip to Step 8, and add a second 856 field for the URL of the second vendor. You should probably add a second copy holdings record, too.

STEP 5: IS THERE A MATCHING RECORD?

Once you've figured out a resource's mode of issuance, how similar resources are handled at your library, and determined it doesn't already have a record in your library's catalog, the next step is to find a MARC Bibliographic record that matches it. Just as you would for a physical resource, you will search for a record in the database of your library's bibliographic utility. Since you may find more than one record that appears to match the resource you are cataloging, it is important to choose a record that is a good match for the resource, and contains the most accurate, complete information.

When looking for a matching record for an e-book, you will probably come across a "provider-neutral" record. Because a single online electronic resource may be distributed by multiple vendors, and could therefore have multiple records in a bibliographic utility's database (one for each vendor), the Program for Cooperative (PCC) has made it their policy to create just one record (a provider-neutral record) for any given online e-resource. The most noticeable thing about these records is that they have multiple 856 (URL) fields, one for each vendor that provides access to the resource. It is perfectly fine to use a provider-neutral record, but do take care to delete all 856 fields that don't direct to the vendor providing the resource to your library.

Here are match points for the most common online electronic resources. Remember, every one of these must be the same on the resource and in the record, or else the record is not a match.

Match points for e-books

> e-ISBN (MARC field 020)
> Author (MARC fields 100, 245 $c)
> Title (MARC field 245)
> Edition (MARC field 250)
> Publisher (MARC field 260 or 264)
> Physical description (MARC fields 300, 336, 337, 338)

Match points for online electronic serials

> ISSN (MARC field 022)
> Title (MARC field 245)
> Publisher (MARC field 260 or 264)
> Frequency of publication (MARC fixed field Frequency)
> Physical description

Match points for online integrating resources

> Title (MARC field 245)
> Publisher (MARC field 260 or 264)
> Physical description (MARC fields 300, 336, 337, 338)
> 856 (URL) (for free websites only)

STEP 6: WHICH RECORD IS BEST?

Often a bibliographic utility will have more than one matching record for the same resource. Which one is best? Here are some points to consider when choosing a record.

Are the classification system and subject headings vocabulary the same as those used at your library? For example, if your library uses DDC, you should opt for a record with a Dewey call number over a record with a Library of Congress call number.

Is the content standard used to create the record the same one used at your library? If your library uses AACR2, you would probably prefer an AACR2 record over an RDA record, and vice-versa.

Is a foreign language used in the cataloging description? You should prefer a record in which the descriptive fields are in English.

Is one record more complete than another? A good indicator of completeness is the value in the MARC Encoding Level fixed field. Here are the most common values found in that field:

> blank   Full-level, input by a PCC library
>
> 1   Full-level, material not examined
>
> 2   Less-than-full level, material not examined
>
> 3   Abbreviated level
>
> 4   Core level

5	Partial (preliminary) level
7	Minimal level
8	Prepublication level

If OCLC is your bibliographic utility, you will see a few other codes used in this field:

I	Full-level, input by OCLC participating library
K	Less-than-full level, input by OCLC participating library
L	Full-level, added through a batch process
M	Less-than-full level, added through a batch process

Full-level cataloging is the most desirable, whereas Core and Minimal levels are less desirable.

Other things to look for:

- The records should have a full call number and subject headings.
- All the information in the record should be accurate, but pay special attention to access points.

STEP 7: HOW DO I GET THE RECORD INTO MY CATALOG?

If your vendor provided a MARC record, you will only be working with your ILS to import the record. The details depend on your ILS, but there are a couple of things to be aware of. First, try to find out from the vendor which character encoding format it used when creating the record; it will probably be MARC-8 or UTF-8. You may need to adjust a setting in your ILS to accept the record when you import it. If your vendor sends you a large number of records at the same time, you will probably want to import them through a batch process. Again, how this is done will depend on your ILS.

If your record is coming from your bibliographic utility, you need to bring it into your local ILS. This is done through software provided by your bibliographic utility and software in your ILS. Typically, you will export the record from your bibliographic utility, and then import it into your library's ILS. If your library's acquisitions department has already added a bibliographic record for the resource, you will need to either replace that record or merge your record with it.

STEP 8: HOW SHOULD I EDIT THE RECORD?

You will almost always need to edit at least the 856 field (URL) in a record for an online electronic resource. The 856 fields are usually coded like this:

1st indicator:	4
2nd indicator:	0
Subfield u	URL
Subfield y	Link text
Subfield z	Public note

As explained in chapter 4, library users are allowed to access a library's electronic resources in two ways: by accessing the resource from a recognized IP range, or authenticating themselves through a proxy server. If your library uses a proxy server, you need to add some hypertext to the beginning of the URL to direct patrons to your library's proxy server. For example, if the URL provided by the vendor is:

http://yourvendor.com&NM=12345

you would add a specific string of hypertext for the proxy server. The final URL would be something like:

http://libezp.zzzu.edu:2048/login?url=http://yourvendor.com&NM=
12345

You may also wish to add a subfield y to create a clickable hotlink, for example, "Click here." Some libraries also add a public note in subfield z, for example, "Available for Zachary Z. Zebulon University patrons only." An 856 field edited to include the above examples would look like this:

856| 4 0 | $u http://libezp.zzzu.edu:2048/login?url=http://
yourvendor.com&NM=12345 $y Click here to access.
$z Available for Zachary Z. Zebulon University patrons only.

In the catalog, it would look like this:

Click here to access. Available for Zachary Z. Zebulon
University patrons only.

You may also wish to change entries for names, some titles, and subject terms to match their preferred forms. This is a form of authority work, and is discussed in more depth in chapter 7.

STEP 9: WHAT OTHER RECORDS SHOULD I ADD?

Once the bibliographic record is in your ILS, you need to create a copy holdings record for it. Copy holdings records give detailed information about what
a library has in its collection. This helps patrons know what a library has,
and helps library staff keep track of the collection. The copy holdings record
for electronic resources usually includes the call number and a location code.
Item records are not typically created for electronic resources because there
is no physical item to keep track of.

STEP 10: HOW DO I KNOW LIBRARY USERS
CAN ACCESS THE RESOURCE?

Once the catalog record has been created, patrons should be able to use it
to access the resource it represents. To ensure that access to the resource
works properly, the authors recommend testing the link in the 856 field. For
IP-authenticated access, all you need to do to test it is click on the link and
confirm it takes you to the correct resource (assuming you are in the IP range
designated for access). For resources that are authenticated both via IP and
proxy authentication, testing access is a little more difficult, because you will
be automatically authenticated because of your IP address. You will need to
test access from a remote location (e.g., from your home), or simulate remote
access through a specially configured computer. Your systems department
may be able to help you with this. If you run into authentication problems,
check the 856 field carefully for any encoding errors. Just one wrong character can create havoc with online access to a resource.

Quality Control

Basic quality control is typically conducted in physical processing, but many
libraries also have a special quality control workflow for cataloging. This may
be as simple as requiring every cataloger to carefully double-check her work,
or as complicated as sending resources (and records) to other catalogers to
review and fill out detailed forms when errors are made. Some cataloging
units do spot checks, for example, looking at one out of every ten records a
cataloger works on. Others conduct in-depth quality control for new catalogers as a part of the learning process. In general, copy cataloging is subject to

less scrutiny than original cataloging. Keep in mind that cataloging errors are inevitable, but they should be kept to a minimum.

Outsourced Cataloging

Some libraries choose to outsource all or part of their cataloging. The most common reasons are a lack of staff resources and a lack of local expertise. The most common form of outsourcing is having your library materials vendor provide catalog records for the materials you purchase from it. If you choose to get catalog records from your vendor, you may have options about what kinds of records you get, and which resources you get records for. For example, you may choose to receive MARC records for firm orders but not for materials supplied through approval plans; only for materials in languages that no catalogers at your library can read; only for resources with certain content; or only when records of a certain quality can be provided. You may even choose to have a materials vendor send resources to you "shelf-ready," that is, fully cataloged and processed, with property stamps, spine labels, and security tags. Vendor-supplied MARC records are usually supplied in batches instead of one by one. The vendor should either send you files via e-mail or provide instructions for retrieving them online. Your ILS should have a mechanism for importing large batches of records.

If you are considering outsourcing, here are some things to think about. Compare the cost of having records supplied to the cost of cataloging in-house. Keep in mind that original catalog records will cost more than copy catalog records. Quality is another concern: get some sample records from the vendor and look them over carefully before you commit to outsourcing. Indicators of quality are: full-level cataloging (this is indicated by the Encoding Level fixed field in MARC); complete call numbers and subject headings, and records that do not require any cleanup editing. When negotiating with a vendor about supplying MARC records, it is wise to inquire about whether, and to what degree, the vendor can customize the records. For example, catalogers might ask a vendor to delete certain MARC fields, or add a library's proxy server prefix to URLs for online resources. Catalogers may also request that the records use a particular MARC character encoding set.

Outsourcing your cataloging does not mean that you no longer need to devote any staff time to cataloging. You should do at least minimal checks of outsourced catalog records, especially when you are just starting to outsource to a vendor. Be assertive about letting the vendor know about any problems you see, and make sure it fixes them.

Outsourcing your library's cataloging can be a godsend, but it is an added expense, takes time and energy to set up, and requires follow-through. If you are thoughtful when setting up an outsourcing program, and do the necessary checking, it can work very well for you.

Trends and Issues in Cataloging

Like other areas of the library, cataloging is always changing, and catalogers are constantly adjusting to changes in technology and in the cataloging world. Following are some significant changes already occurring, or on the horizon for cataloging.

In a departure from the traditional practice of cataloging one resource at a time, catalogers are increasingly working with large files made up of many MARC records. These records may come from a vendor concurrent with access to e-books, or they may be the way outsourced catalog records are supplied. This work involves a higher level of computer skills than traditional cataloging. It often means working with the ILS's server and administrative functions, and editing batches of records with special MARC editing software.

Many libraries are undertaking projects to digitize unique materials they hold (especially archival resources), and make the digitized images and documents available online. These resources are described with metadata records, a kind of structured information that is shorter and less complicated than traditional cataloging records. *Metadata* literally means "data about data." Catalog records are considered a kind of metadata, but in libraries the term is used to mean a simplified way of describing resources that uses different and fewer rules. Strict adherence to international standards is less important for metadata record creation because the materials described are unique, and therefore the records aren't shared between institutions. Metadata specialists must make choices about what information to include in metadata records, and what controlled vocabulary or vocabularies to use. Because metadata creation is similar to cataloging, many catalogers find themselves learning about metadata and using it to describe digitized resources.

Another significant development is the Bibliographic Framework Initiative (BIBFRAME), an effort to create a successor to the MARC format. Although MARC is a very sturdy and reliable data format standard, it is now almost fifty years old, and hasn't kept up with current computer technology. MARC records were designed to be manipulated by computers, but the textual content of the fields can only be read and understood by humans. The World Wide Web is increasingly made up of "linked data"—that is, data that is not just manipulated but actually understood by computers. The way it works is by parsing data into small pieces that are linked in a language-like structure. BIBFRAME is being developed to take advantage of linked data, and therefore make library information more like the interconnected data on the World Wide Web.

Every once in a while, some expert declares that cataloging is obsolete. The facts don't support this notion. Many catalogers have added metadata creation to their job duties, while others find themselves quite busy creating original records for digital resources and self-published books. Cataloging is certainly changing, but it is still vital for helping library patrons find the resources they want.

Final Thoughts

Cataloging is a complex process, due to the many rules and standards that catalogers use so they can share records with each other. Because there is so much technical information used in creating catalog records, you won't remember everything. Fortunately, there are many free websites for cataloging information, as well as some that are available by subscription. One of the most helpful is Cataloger's Desktop, a large compendium of useful cataloging documentation available by subscription from the Library of Congress.

The cooperative spirit of cataloging extends to a willingness to help new catalogers. Here are some e-mail lists that welcome questions from new catalogers:

AutoCAT is a long-running e-mail list for catalogers of all kinds of materials (https://listserv.syr.edu/scripts/wa.exe?A0=AUTOCAT).

OCLC-CAT is one of many e-mail lists maintained by OCLC (www3.oclc .org/app/listserv).

OLAC-L is part of the Online Audiovisual Catalogers, and a wonderful place to ask questions about cataloging AV materials (http://olacinc .org/drupal/?q=node/57).

Cataloging is learned through practice and (inevitably) mistakes. Don't be discouraged if it seems overwhelming at first. There is a lot to master, but you really can learn it. Take your time, look up things you don't know, and ask questions of other catalogers. You may be surprised to find, as many an accidental cataloger has, that you enjoy cataloging much more than you thought you would. Finally, remember that the reason for cataloging is to help library users find resources they need, so keep them in mind as you make every cataloging decision.

Resources

Bibliographic Framework Initiative. www.loc.gov/bibframe.

Cataloger's Desktop. Washington, DC: Library of Congress, 2014. www.desk top.loc.gov.

Ercelawn, Ann. Tools for Serials Catalogers. 1995. www.library.vanderbilt .edu/ercelawn/serials.html.

Kaplan, Allison. *Crash Course in Cataloging for Non-Catalogers.* Westport, CT: Libraries Unlimited, 2009.

Kaplan, Allison, and Ann Riedling. *Catalog It: A Guide to Cataloging School Library Materials.* 2nd ed. Worthington, OH: Linworth Publishing, 2006.

Linked Data—Connect Distributed Data across the Web. www.linkeddata .org.

Lubas, Rebecca. "Managing Vendor Cataloging to Maximize Access." In *Practical Strategies for Cataloging Departments,* edited by Rebecca L. Lubas, 65–72. Santa Barbara: Libraries Unlimited, 2011.

Weihs, Jean, and Sheila S. Intner. *Beginning Cataloging.* Santa Barbara: Libraries Unlimited, 2009.

6

Physical Processing

What is the purpose of physical processing? After the library's staff has gone to so much trouble to develop selection lists, decide what to buy, place the order, receive it, and catalog it, identifying the materials as belonging to your library and being able to find them on the shelf is probably a good idea. To do that, physically marking each item in some way is necessary.

In general, physical processing consists of placing a call number label, property stamps, security target, and (rarely) packaging. Physical processing may occur in different parts of the workflow in technical services. Property stamps and security strips or targets can be placed as new materials are checked in, or as they are labeled. Depending on your workflow, physical processing can also include adding item records to the ILS, placing bar code labels, quality assurance, and updating the item status as an item heads out of technical services. In some libraries, the physical processing unit also handles materials repair, cleaning, and conservation. However, because this is outside the immediate scope of this book, it will not be addressed in detail.

As with everything else in the library, what physical processing is done varies with the material format; those differences will be addressed in specific sections in this chapter. However, to start with, let's take a closer look at each of the steps of physical processing.

This chapter will cover:

- Call number placement
- Bar code placement
- Property stamps

- Security
- Packaging
- Processing by format
- Quality control
- Trends and issues in physical processing

Before You Begin

Think about the comparative costs of various levels of physical processing versus the cost of the item. If the cost of the processing is more than the cost of the item, you may want to add or skip steps.

Specialized Terms

Bar code label—An adhesive label with a bar code on it. Used for linking the item with the record.

Call number label—An adhesive label that displays call number information on or around the spine of a book.

Conservation—The process of maintaining, mending, and cleaning an item.

Ephemera—Materials with a short lifetime. This includes mass market paperbacks, pamphlets, brochures, and other materials that either break down or are useful for only a limited time.

Mending—The process of repairing materials.

Mylar covers—Clear book jackets made out of Mylar plastic put over the dust jackets of hardback books. They extend the life of the dust jacket and any information printed on it.

Property stamp—An ink stamp that usually includes the name of the owning library and other information as desired.

RFID—Radio frequency identification, a type of materials security system.

Security systems—Any of various systems used to control a collection so it cannot be removed from the building without setting
off an alarm.

Signature—Two or more sheets of paper folded together as a prelimi-
nary step for binding. Used primarily in hardback books.

Spine label—Another name for the call number label.

Call Number Placement

Placing a call number label, also called a spine label, on an item allows for
ease of shelving and locating items on the shelves. Towards this end, you
want to make sure that the placement allows for easy viewing of the label.
Although call numbers can be placed anywhere on an item, for maximum
visibility, they will usually be placed towards the bottom of the spine if there
is enough space. If not, they are often placed in the lower-left corner of the
front of the item (see figure 6.1).

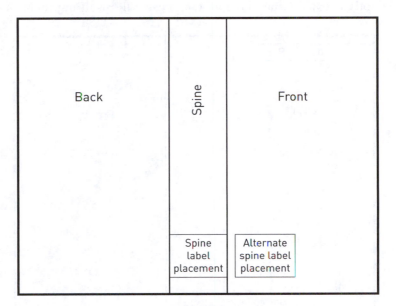

FIGURE 6.1
Spine label placement

Avoid the following:

Centering the label horizontally on the spine. This results in only the middle section of longer numbers being visible, making them very difficult to find on the shelf.

Wrapping the spine label around the spine. If the label is wider than the spine, it is better to trim it to size than to wrap it around. By wrapping it around, the unused portion is abraded each time the book is taken on or off the shelf, which will lead to the label being peeled off in time.

Bar Code Placement

Most libraries use specialized bar codes for circulation, inventory, and materials tracking. These are like the UPC codes you see on most goods currently sold in the United States. In libraries, each bar code is unique and, in most cases, identifies a specific item. Where to place the bar code on a resource has been a hotly debated issue in the past, and can still result in problems when

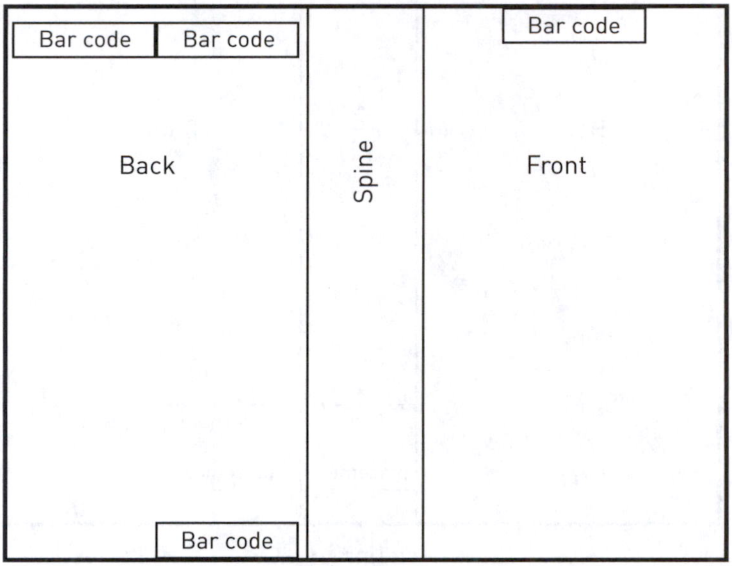

FIGURE 6.2
Bar code placement

changes to various systems in the library make it necessary to change the placement of the bar code. An example of a system that can affect bar code placement is if the library adds a self-checkout system that requires bar codes to be placed in the center of the front of the book. Rebarcoding an entire collection is an expensive proposition that can tie up library resources, staff, and equipment for some time.

The requirements of any self-checkout system in use should be considered when deciding where to place a bar code label. Placing the bar code on the inside of the item means that it probably won't be lost or defaced, but adds an extra step by requiring circulation staff to open the item to access the bar code label. Placing the bar code on the outside of the item makes the workflow at circulation easier, but also makes it easier for the bar code to be defaced or peeled off. (See figure 6.2.)

Property Stamps

Property stamps serve a couple of different purposes. They identify which library owns the item and, if necessary, which location the item belongs in. They can also serve as part of the security of an item. Placement can vary quite a bit based on the format of the item as well as the design of the item.

Security

Security systems are needed to keep library materials from just walking out the door, never to return. There are several types; the one you choose will depend on the format of the item being secured.

One of the oldest security systems is an identifying mark placed somewhere on the item where it will not be easily noticed. Another variation of this is to put a property stamp on a particular page number of every book. While this does not stop the item from walking out the door, it does make it easier to identify the materials if they appear in used book stores later. As the variety of formats has increased, so has the need for different types of security. In the past, a library would put property stamps in odd places in books, engrave its name on vinyl records in the area around the spindle hole, or write it on the edges of filmstrips. With the advent of electronic security systems, libraries moved to a variety of magnetic tags and strips, which

continued advancing with each new materials format until the advent of
radio frequency identification (RFID) systems for libraries in the 1990s.

One big decision for a library is whether it even needs a security system
and, if so, what kind it should be. Security systems are fairly expensive to
install, especially in an existing building. A cost-benefit analysis is a good
tool to determine whether to proceed. It compares the costs of the system,
such as installation, start-up expenses, ongoing expenses, and staff resources,
to the estimated amount you will save by not having to replace lost and sto-
len materials. Much of the work of implementing a security system may fall
to technical services staff, who will be responsible for tagging the current collection and new materials as they come in.

What Is a Library Materials Security System?

Library materials security systems are similar to the anti-theft systems used
in retail stores. They are designed to sound an alarm or otherwise notify library
staff if an item is being removed from the building without being checked out.

Security measures have evolved over time. In medieval libraries, books were
actually chained to desks so they could not be removed. In more recent times,
libraries stationed staff at exit doors to check bags for materials. In the 1970s,
the 3M Corporation introduced the first materials security system, which is still
in use today. Over the past forty or so years, three basic systems have come
into widespread use. These are electromagnetic (EM), radio frequency (RF),
and radio frequency identification (RFID). Although they all work on different
premises, they do have some things in common.

All three of these library materials security systems are based on two parts.
The first is a target located in the item and the second is a sensor or scanner,
usually in the form of a gate. Because the scanner requires a matching target
on every library resource, the decision to install a new security system should
be thought out very carefully. Re-tagging an entire collection when you change
systems is neither cheap nor easy.

When Do You Need One?

Not all libraries need a security system. If you can't document that materials
are walking out your door without being checked out, you probably don't need
one. Smaller libraries with low traffic and only one entrance probably don't need

one, because the person checking things out can probably monitor whatever traffic there is. Libraries with very limited patron bases probably don't need one either, because the small number of people using the library makes it easier to maintain the security of the collection. It's important to make sure you actually need a security system before you invest in one.

How Do They Work?

Electromagnetic (EM) systems work by inserting a magnetized tag or target that can be sensitized or desensitized on the book, CD, DVD, magazine, or other resource. Sensitization and desensitization are accomplished by rubbing a large handheld magnet over the item, placing the item in a cradle which passes the target over a strong magnet, or running the item through a strong magnetic field.

Radio frequency (RF) systems work by placing a low-frequency radio antenna in the item. These antennae are already "turned on" when purchased, and are often hidden in date-due card pockets. The system works by interrupting (turning off) the radio antenna by inserting a detuning card over the target. A system is tuned to one of a variety of frequencies allowed by the Federal Communications Commission (FCC), so there is a chance that materials from one library won't necessarily work with another RF security system. This can be an issue with interlibrary loan materials or in multi-site library systems.

The newest library security system to enter common usage is *radio frequency identification (RFID).* Built on many of the same principles as RF technology, library RFID systems are the same as those used for inventory control in retail stores and keyless-lock mechanisms. Rather than being a simple antenna, the target in an RFID system is a transponder that, when read, provides information about the item it is attached to, including whether or not it is checked out, bar code number, and author/title.

Advantages and Disadvantages

Each system has advantages and disadvantages. Note that this is not a comprehensive list but just a jumping-off point for some of the issues that you will need to consider if you are looking at implementing or changing your security system.

EM Systems

The big advantage of EM systems is their affordability. The targets are fairly inexpensive and easy to apply. They are also generic, so you don't need to add information to each tag about the resource it is attached to. Another advantage is flexibility—targets have been designed for most formats being actively collected by modern libraries. These targets are also fairly unobtrusive, so it is easy to place them so they cannot be easily found and removed. EM systems are also compatible with self-checkout units that automatically desensitize materials that are placed in a cradle to have their bar codes scanned.

There are several disadvantages of EM systems. These include the need for special equipment to sensitize and desensitize magnetically based formats such as VHS and cassette tapes, which could be erased. There are also some limitations on where gates can be installed, because they must be a certain distance from computer equipment and metal door frames. Older systems can also affect heart pacemakers, hearing aids, and other medical equipment based on either computer or magnetic technologies. Another issue with EM gates is that they can be set off by some types of belt buckles and piercing jewelry.

RF Systems

One advantage of RF systems is that they are safe to use with all formats, including audio- and videotape. They also do not require the extra circulation steps of sensitizing and desensitizing materials each time they are returned or checked out. Although RF gates must be installed away from computer equipment and metal doorways, the distance is less than with EM systems. In addition, the targets are affordable and easy to place.

A disadvantage is that a physical de-tuner must be placed in each book to desensitize it to the alarm. This makes RF systems poor candidates for self-checkout systems. Also, the targets, especially on non-circulating materials, are fairly obvious and easy to remove.

RFID Systems

The big advantage of RFID systems is the flexibility and usefulness of the system. With a fully installed and implemented RFID system, your staff can scan a shelf with a wand to read the RFID tags and do inventory, shelf reading, and a host of other activities with minimal added work. RFID is ideally suited for self-checkout systems, because the information on the transponder is read when you run the book through the check-out station. RFID also takes the place of bar codes, which eliminates another step in physical processing.

The main disadvantage is the cost. RFID tags are by far the most expensive tags to buy. They also require staff to create a link between the tag and a computer record. The reading systems and gates for RFID are also more expensive that those required for either EM or RF systems.

Conclusion

Once the decision to implement a materials security system is made, there are many factors that go into selection of the appropriate system. All systems are fairly expensive to get up and running, so the decision needs to be very well thought out before you begin implementation. Switching systems can be even more expensive. Factors including budget, physical space, and the long term needs and usefulness of the system all need to be evaluated. However, in libraries where they are needed, materials security systems can save thousands of dollars every year in missing materials.

Packaging

Some materials need to be repackaged before they go out for circulation. These can include kits, read-along packages, some DVDs and CDs, and resources with accompanying materials. Packaging can run from custom-made boxes to hanging bags to shelf placeholders for materials that must be requested from the desk. Repackaging is usually only necessary when an item has multiple parts that need to be kept together, or if the packaging an item was received in is not suitable for library circulation.

Processing by Format

Now come the nuts and bolts of processing requirements by format. The particular steps you will follow for each format will depend on your library. Determine what your local practices are. Don't hesitate to ask why your library does something, because if you can eliminate even one step that no longer serves a purpose, you will make your process more efficient.

Periodicals

After periodicals are received or checked in, they need to be processed before setting them out on the shelf for use. To process them, you will usually:

1. Place a date stamp on the item showing when it was received.

2. Place a property stamp on the item showing which institution owns it.

3. If your institution has a security system, tag the item.

4. If your institution uses them, place an informational label on the issue showing title, issue date, volume number, and issue number. This information is helpful for people who use your periodical collection for research and staff who maintain the periodical collection.

Keep two things in mind when choosing where to position identifying information. First, do not cover any useful information. Patrons will be frustrated if they are not able to read information that has been covered by labels. It is also important not to make editorial comments through the placement of stamps and/or labels, such as strategically placing the label on *Sports Illustrated*'s Swimsuit Edition, or stamping the face of a politician featured on the cover of a weekly news magazine. Second, place stamps, labels, strips, and so forth in places where it will be difficult to remove them. This will discourage patrons from walking off with materials.

Books

There are three different physical book formats: *hardback, trade paperback,* and *mass market paperback*. In many libraries, each physical format is handled differently.

First, let's review steps that will be common to all books.

1. Print call number labels as needed.

2. Check the item for damage or binding errors.

3. Apply call number labels as needed, preferably to the spine, or to the lower-left front corner if the spine is not wide enough.

4. Place appropriate property stamps. These will most often go on the top edge of the text block and on the title page.

5. Place the bar code sticker in the desired location, if it hasn't already been applied earlier in the process.

6. Place a security strip or target in an appropriate location. Where to place the strip or target depends on the style you are using. The

most common are double-sided strips in the gutter of the book, or targets integrated with the bar code or on the front or back end-papers. Remember that the objective is to not cover up any useful information.

Additional steps for hardbacks can include:

1. Applying Mylar covers to the book jackets.
2. Attaching Mylar covers to the book either by glue or tape.

Note that if your library does not keep the dust jackets on hardbacks, they will usually have been removed and discarded before the materials reach physical processing. If your library does keep the dust jackets, it is usually better to apply call number and bar code labels to the dust jacket before the Mylar cover is attached, rather than placing them on the Mylar cover, while security strips and/or targets should be attached directly to the book.

Additional steps for trade paperbacks may include:

1. Applying reinforcing tape to the spine.
2. Applying protective tape over the call number label and the bar code.

Mass market paperbacks tend to be handled differently. Most libraries treat them as ephemera, or materials that will only be popular or used for a short time and so do not invest the time in complete cataloging for them. Indeed, in many libraries they are added to "generic" paperback records. As such, the level of processing they receive can vary widely from library to library, even within the same system.

An additional step for mass market paperbacks may be to apply reinforcing tape to the spine.

Audiovisual (AV) Materials

Physically processing the variety of media formats can be challenging, because they each have different requirements. Although compact discs and DVD/Blu-ray style formats are most common today, many libraries still have collections of older media formats (VHS, cassettes, etc.), and newer formats are still being introduced. For example, as of this writing, the library where the authors work just added a book on a flash drive, because the publisher refused permission to load it to a server. However, this discussion will focus on compact disc style formats (CDs, DVDs, Blu-ray, etc.) because they are the most common.

The following steps need to be followed for all AV formats:

1. Print call number labels, as needed.

2. Check the item for damage to both the media and the packaging. This may include playing the media.

3. If needed, apply call number labels, preferably to the spine, but to the lower-left front corner if the spine is not wide enough.

4. Place appropriate property stamps. These will most often be on the front of the cover, which may require disassembling the packaging, and any inserts included with the item. Some discs will accept a property stamp on the front of the item itself. However, this will not work with double-sided media or discs that ink does not adhere to.

5. Write the bar code number in indelible ink around the spindle hole of the disc. Do *not* write in the information-bearing area of the disc.

6. Place the bar code in the desired location, if it hasn't already been applied.

7. Choose from the available options for placing security strips on audiovisual media. The best, and most expensive, is a "doughnut" containing a target that is applied to the non-playable side of the disc. These must be placed very carefully or the disc will not play. Placing book style targets in the case can also work. The advantage is that you do not risk rendering the media unplayable by attaching it. The disadvantage is that this doesn't stop people from removing the media from the case and walking out with it.

Another option is tamper resistant or anti-theft packaging as used in many stores. These include various types of large plastic frames that make it harder to secret a disc out of the library, and various types of locking mechanisms for individual cases. These types of packaging do help decrease theft without risking the integrity of the media. However, they have several downsides, including cost, increased storage space per item, and additional steps and staff time at circulation.

A final option is to forego security for media and only display the empty packaging, and keep the media itself in a secure place, usually behind the circulation desk. Although cheaper in terms of supplies and processing time, this requires more storage space and staff time at circulation.

Quality Control

The final step of physical processing is quality control. The item going out to the shelf must be cataloged and labeled correctly so staff can shelve it appropriately and patrons can find it.

The steps of quality control are:

1. Check the physical item. Although this should have been done during receiving and physical processing, do a final check to make sure all parts are there, in good condition, the disc and the packaging match, the text block is bound correctly, etc.
2. Check the catalog record. Make sure it matches the item in hand.
3. Check the item record. Make sure bar code numbers, location codes, and other information are correct.
4. Check all labeling and property stamps.
5. For periodicals, make sure the volume/number/date on the label (if used) matches the item.

You usually don't need to check 100 percent of the items passing through technical services on their way to the public. Materials put out by new staff should be checked more closely, as should formats not handled on a regular basis. In most cases, spot-checking a few items will suffice.

Trends and Issues in Physical Processing

As the use of digital materials increases, the need for physical processing will decrease.

RFID technology is becoming more prevalent. This technology combines security and bar code into one target, rather than a target and a label. The need to reprocess the existing collection and the cost of the targets has limited the growth of RFID. However, as prices come down, this will change.

As part of the wider library trend of doing more with less, there is a continuing movement towards the implementation of self-checkout systems in many libraries. These systems allow patrons to check materials out for themselves. However, to enable self-checkout, bar codes are applied in very specific places, depending on the self-checkout device being used. As self-checkout becomes more prevalent, physical processing will need to change the placement of bar codes on new materials and reprocess older materials.

Finally, the trend towards outsourcing cataloging and processing in favor of receiving shelf-ready materials is affecting physical processing. Libraries will always need to do some physical processing in house, but as more libraries move to shelf-ready programs, the amount of physical processing will decrease, freeing staff for other functions.

Final Thoughts

Physical processing is the last step in the process to get materials from the vendor to your patrons. Too often, it is the part of the process given the least amount of thought, and is relegated to students, volunteers, or lower-level staff. Remember that a poorly processed item might be hard to find, may not stand up well to repeated circulations, and in the long run will become some of the most expensive materials libraries have on their shelves.

Resources

Bailey, Timothy P., Amanda L. Scott, and Rickey D. Best. "Cost Differentials between E-Books and Print in Academic Libraries." *College & Research Libraries* 76, no. 1 (2015): 6–18.

Kesner, Richard. "Conservation and Community Action: Bringing the Message Home." *Georgia Archive* 7, no. 2 (2014): 42–46.

"Introduction to Book Repair." Lansing, MI: Library of Michigan, 2001. http://michigan.gov/documents/hal/book_repair_handouts_251280_7.doc.

Spidal, D. F. "Physical Processing of Monographs by Library Technical Services. *Library Collections, Acquisitions, & Technical Service* 35 (January 2011): 1–9.

Walker, M., and D. Kulczak. "Shelf-Ready Books Using PromptCat and YBP: Issues to Consider (An Analysis of Errors at the University of Arkansas)." *Library Collections, Acquisitions, & Technical Services* 31 (February 2007): 61–84.

Authority Control and Catalog Maintenance

Authority control and catalog maintenance fall outside the main technical services workflow, but each is important to maintain the usefulness of the catalog for library users and library staff alike. Because both involve making corrections to catalog records, and use similar tools, they are often done by the same person or group.

This chapter will cover:

- Authority control
- Catalog maintenance
- Trends and issues in authority control and catalog maintenance

Before You Begin

Authority control and catalog maintenance can be time-consuming processes that require special expertise and skills. Before delving into authority control and catalog maintenance at your library, here are some questions to answer:

- Does your library do authority control?
    If so, does it outsource authority control?
    If not, what processes are followed?
- What set of subject terms is used at your library?
- What kinds of reports are available through your ILS?

Specialized Terms

Access point—A searchable unit of information in a catalog record.

Analysis—The process of cataloging the parts of a resource separately, with each part having its own record.

Authority file—A database made up of individual authority records.

Authority record—A MARC record that records the preferred form of a name, title, or subject term; includes variant forms ("see" and "see also" references) and citations for the sources used to make the decision about the preferred form.

Collocation—The process of bringing resources together that have the same author, subject, classification, or series title.

Corporate body—An organization that has a name and acts as one entity.

Cross-reference—A reference from one heading to another.

Disambiguation—In authority work, the process of differentiating one name, title, or subject term from another.

Heading—A kind of access point. A heading can be a personal name, a corporate body name, a title, or a subject term.

"See also" reference—A cross-reference that refers users from one preferred form of a name, title, or subject to a related preferred form of a name, title, or subject term.

"See" reference—A cross-reference that refers users from a variant form of a name, title, or subject term to the preferred term.

Series title—The title given to a group of related individual resources that have the same publisher and are issued over time.

Tracing—The process of recording the preferred form, or heading, of a piece of information in a bibliographic record.

Uniform title—the preferred form of a title, usually a series title or the title of a classic work of literature or music.

Authority Control

As discussed in chapter 5, every bibliographic record contains access points—units of information that are searchable in the library's catalog. A library catalog can contain thousands or even millions of access points, including call numbers, ISBNs, titles of resources, personal names, corporate body names, series titles, and subject terms. Some access points, such as ISBNs and (usually) call numbers are unique, and found in only one bibliographic record in a catalog. But other access points, such as personal names, series titles, and subject terms are likely to be repeated in more than one record. For example, the name "J. K. Rowling" would appear as an access point in records for all of the books she has written; likewise, records for books about the Brooklyn Bridge would all have a subject term for the Brooklyn Bridge. The form of the name or title in an access point is guided by a content standard.

The practice of authority control was developed to help users make sense of all these repeatable access points. With authority control, one unique form is established for an access point that is likely to be found in multiple records, and that form is used consistently throughout the catalog. Without authority control, catalog records for different books by J. K. Rowling might use different forms of her name, for example, Jo Rowling and Joanne Rowling. If a library user were searching for all books by this author, how would he know to search for all three forms of the name? Fortunately, catalogers work hard to make sure the same form of a name, title, or subject is used consistently in the catalog. This means that most personal and corporate body names, and all subject terms, have one unique "authorized," or preferred, form. Some titles, such as series titles, also have authorized forms. Consistently using one unique, preferred form keeps similar names, subjects, and titles from being confused with each other, and allows every record with that name, subject, or title to be retrieved together with just one search.

For example, when every book by the fiction author Stephen King has "King, Stephen, 1947-" as an access point, records for all of his books may be found with just one search of the catalog; it is also harder to confuse him with the Stephen King ("King, Stephen, 1931-2006") who wrote the marketing book *Developing New Brands*.

This example illustrates the two major principles of authority control: disambiguation and collocation.

Disambiguation means making the preferred form of every name, title, and subject term both unique and different from similar names, titles, or subject terms. Similar names and titles are made different from each other (disambiguated) by adding additional pieces of information called qualifiers. The most common qualifiers for personal names are birth dates, death dates, and fuller forms of the name. For example, "Thomas Stearns" is a qualifier added to the preferred form of the name, "Eliot, T. S.," so the final form is: "Eliot, T. S. (Thomas Stearns)." Geographical information is often added to corporate body names to distinguish one from another, for example, "First Baptist Church (Clovis, N.M.)." Series titles are usually differentiated by adding qualifiers for the place of publication or for the organization responsible for their publication, for example: "Dispatches (Fredonia, N.Y.)" and "Bulletin (American Geographical Society)."

 Collocation means grouping together similar resources, for example, everything by the same author or everything with the same subject. The consistent use of authorized forms of names and subject terms makes this possible.

Why Do Authority Control?

The greatest argument in favor of doing authority control is the cost of *not* doing authority control. If catalogers used any old headings they wanted when creating bibliographic records, the library catalog would be chaotic. For example, let's say a cataloger uses the term "Films" as a subject heading for the book *The New York Times Guide to the Best 1,000 Movies Ever Made.* Another cataloger at the same library uses the term "Movies" as a subject heading for *TCM Classic Movie Trivia*, while yet another uses "Moving pictures" as a subject term for *Fascinating Facts about Classic Movies.* How would a library user know which subject terms to use to find these books in the catalog? The answer is: she wouldn't, and she might waste a lot of time trying to find books on the topic. Library personnel would also have trouble locating these items in the catalog. Besides wasting the time of library patrons and staff, a disorganized catalog reflects poorly on a library. If someone from a library's funding agency has a frustrating time trying to work with a messy catalog, it could jeopardize funding for the library. Not practicing authority control can cost a library monetarily, too. If a library with a disorganized catalog wants to join a consortium of other libraries, it may be required to pay to bring its catalog into compliance with authority control practices at the consortium. Finally, a lack of authority control may increase the cost of migrating to a new ILS.

Authority Control and Bibliographic Records

The preferred form recorded in an authority record is the form to be used in any bibliographic record including that name, title, or subject term as an access point. When the form in the bibliographic record matches the preferred form in the authority record, the heading in the bibliographic record is said to be "authorized," or "valid."

The following access points in bibliographic records are subject to authority control:

Personal names: MARC fields 100, 600, 700, 800 (X00)

Corporate body names: MARC fields 110, 610, 710, 810 (X10)

Conference/Meeting names: MARC fields 111, 611, 711, 811 (X11)

Uniform titles: MARC fields 130, 630, 730, 830 (X30)

Topical subject terms: MARC field 650

Geographical subject terms: MARC field 651

In the case of names and uniform titles, the MARC field in which an access point is recorded indicates its role in the bibliographic record. That is, any personal name, corporate body name, conference name, or uniform title can be given as the main access point, an added access point or a subject heading in a bibliographic record.

For example, the record for a book *written by* Malcolm Gladwell would have "Gladwell, Malcolm, 1963-" in a MARC 100 field; the record for a book *edited by* Malcolm Gladwell would have his name in a MARC 700 field; and the record for a book *about* Malcolm Gladwell would have his name in a MARC 600 field.

The record for a book *by* Goodwill Industries of America would have that name in a 110 field; the record for a book that Goodwill Industries of America *helped create* would have that name in a 710 field, and the record for a book *about* Goodwill Industries of America would have that name in a 610 field.

Authority Files

Just as a library has a local catalog made up of bibliographic records, it has a local authority file made up of individual authority records. Each authority record represents the preferred or authorized form of a name, title, or subject term. Authority records are encoded in the MARC Authorities format. The records in a local authority file are copies of records in a national authority file, a giant repository of authority records, each of them unique. In the United States, the national authority file is maintained by the Library of Congress (http://authorities.loc.gov). A library's local authority file typically includes a record for every subject term in the controlled vocabulary used at the library, but only those name and title authority records needed to support headings found in the library's catalog. Any record in a local authority file should match the record for that same name, title, or subject term in the national authority file, with the exception of any authority records that are created locally and only exist in the local authority file. Since the cataloging standard used at the Library of Congress is *Resource Description and Access* (RDA), the name and title records in the national authority file follow RDA practice.

Authority Records

The preferred form of a name, title, or subject term is recorded in an authority record. The preferred form is chosen and constructed by a cataloger, following rules found in a content standard. These days, the content standard used for choosing and constructing preferred forms is RDA. In addition to the preferred form of the name, title, or subject term, the authority record usually includes cross-references—variants of the preferred form that might be searched by a patron. The authority file is designed to direct patrons from the variant form to the preferred form. There are two kinds of cross-references: "See references" direct users to the preferred form of the term; "See also references" direct patrons to related headings. Authority records also include citations for the sources used to choose and construct the preferred form.

There are different kinds of authority records for different kinds of preferred terms. The most common are personal name, corporate body name, conference or meeting name, uniform title, topical subject, and geographical place name.

PERSONAL NAMES

When librarian Barbara Olson looks up the music producer Sean Combs (i.e., she enters the search term "Combs, Sean") in the Milwaukee Public Library's catalog, she sees this:

Combs, Sean, 1969-
See: Diddy, 1969-

She is prompted by the "See" reference to click on "Diddy, 1969-." When she does, she retrieves a list of library materials:

Bad Boy's 10th Anniversary: [sound recording] The Hits
2004
Bad Boy Records
In Media Room, CD Area

Duets [sound recording] : The Final Chapter
2005
Bad Boy Records
In Media Room, CD Area

Hop-Hop Laws of Success [videorecording]
2006
Simmons-Lathan Media Group
In Media Room, DVD Area

Why was Barbara directed to search for "Diddy, 1969-," and how? It has to do with the authority record for the person Diddy, and the way that record works in the library's OPAC. Here is the MARC Authority record for Diddy:

100 1	$a Diddy, $d 1969-	
400 1	$a Puff Daddy, $d 1969-	
400 1	$a P. Diddy, $d 1969-	
400 1	$a Combs, Sean, $d 1969-	
400 1	$a Combs, Puffy, $d 1969-	
400 1	$a Puffy, $d 1969-	
400 1	$a Diddy, P., $d 1969-	
400 1	$a Combs, $d 1969-	
400 1	$a Combs, Diddy, $d 1969-	
670	$a Rolling stone, Apr. 20, 1995: $b p. 24 (Sean "Puff Daddy" Combs; rap music producer, owner of Bad Boy Entertainment)	
670	$a All Music Guide WWW site, Jan. 25, 2002 $b (Puff Daddy; Sean "Puffy"Combs; P. Diddy; b. Nov. 4, 1970, Harlem, NY; producer)	
670	$a Dogg Pound (Musical group). Cali iz active [SR] p2006: $b container (Diddy)	

670    $a Wikipedia, July 25, 2006 $b (Sean Combs; Sean Jean Combs; b.
       Nov. 4, 1969; American record producer, actor, and entertainment
       mogul; his current nickname and recording name is Diddy;
       previously, he has been known as Puff Daddy, P. Diddy, and Puffy)

The preferred form of the name, "Diddy, 1969-," is recorded in the 100 field.
This is the "authorized" form of the name, the form that should appear in the
100, 600, or 700 field in a bibliographic record. The variant form of the name,
"Combs, Sean, 1969-," is recorded in a 400 field. When Barbara searched for
the name "Combs, Sean," the 400 field prompted the OPAC to display a "See"
reference directing her to the preferred form of the name and providing a link
to it. If Barbara had searched by "Puff Daddy," "P. Diddy," or any of the other
variant names in the authority record (any of the 400 fields), she would still
have been directed to the preferred form of the name, "Diddy, 1969-." You
may remember that in MARC Bibliographic, tags for personal names all end in
-00. MARC Authority tags work the same way. The preferred form of the name
is recorded in a 100 field, and the variant forms are recorded in 400 fields.

The 670 fields give sources the cataloger who created the authority record
used to construct the preferred and variant forms of the name. 670 fields are
not searchable in the OPAC, and are generally present only for the use of
catalogers.

CORPORATE BODY NAMES

In cataloging terms, a corporate body is an organization that has a name and
acts as one entity. Corporations, parts of government, musical groups, and
theater companies—as far as catalogers are concerned, they are all corporate
bodies. This is the authority record from the national authority file for the
corporation Apple Computer:

110 2 $a Apple Computer, Inc.
410 2 $a Apple (Firm)
670     $a Price, J. How to write a computer manual, c1984: $b CIP t.p.
        (Apple Computer, Inc.)
670     $a The High-Tech marketing companion, 1993: $b CIP galley
        (Apple)

Note that the preferred and variant forms of the name are in 110 and 410
fields. Just like the MARC tags in a bibliographic record, corporate body
names appear in fields that end in -10. As in a personal name authority

record, the 670 fields give the information the cataloger used to decide on the preferred and variant forms of the name.

CONFERENCE/MEETING NAMES

Conferences, conventions, trade shows and fairs are a kind of corporate body. Here is the authority record from the national authority file for the American Library Association's Midwinter Conference:

> 111 2 $a ALA Midwinter Meeting
>
> 411 2 $a ALA Midwinter Conference
>
> 410 2 $a American Library Association. $b Midwinter meeting
>
> 670 $a Its (1991: Chicago, Ill.). Think tank on the present and future of the online catalog, 1991: $b t.p. (ALA Midwinter Meeting)
>
> 670 $a The Future is now, 1994: $b t.p. (ALA Midwinter Conference)

Notice that the acronym "ALA" is used instead of "American Library Association." When a cataloger chooses the preferred form of a name, it is based on the way the name most frequently appears in published materials. In this case, the cataloger determined that "ALA" is used more often than "American Library Association" in publications about the midwinter conference, so she used that form in the preferred form of the conference name. The preferred and variant forms of the conference name are in MARC fields that end in -11, just like entries for conferences in MARC Bibliographic records. The organization organizing the conference, the American Library Association, is given in a 410 field, with the Midwinter Meeting given as a subunit of the organization. This is for anyone who might look up the conference using "ALA"—the 410 field is a "See" reference that will direct him to the preferred form of the conference name. Finally, just as in personal name and corporate name authority records, the 670 fields give the resources used to create the preferred and variant forms of the conference name.

UNIFORM TITLES

A uniform title is simply the preferred form of a title. Uniform titles are created for the titles of series; for works that are likely to be republished, such as classic works of literature; and for works that are performed and recorded time and again, such as classical music compositions. This section will present examples and discuss each kind of uniform title.

Here is the authority record from the national authority file for a series title:

130 0 $a Amazing Americans (Teacher Created Materials, Inc.)

643     $a Huntington Beach, CA $b Teacher Created Materials

644     $a f

645     $a t

646     $a s

670     $a Kemp, Kristin. Thurgood Marshall, 2015: $b title page (Amazing Americans)

The preferred form of the series title is given in the 130 field, and the publisher and place of publication are given in the 643 field.

The 644, 645, and 646 fields give guidance about how the series is to be treated. As discussed in chapter 5, sometimes a series is treated like a serial; other times each part of a series has its own catalog record. When each part has its own record, the series is said to be "analyzed." The code in MARC field 644, subfield a ("f") indicates the series is analyzed. The code in MARC field 645, subfield a ("t") gives guidance about "tracing" the series title. This means that the preferred form of the series title should appear in an 830 field in the bibliographic record for each part of the series. For example, the bibliographic record for the book *Amazing Americans: Rosa Parks* would look something like this (we're only giving some of the MARC fields):

100 1 $a Kemp, Kristin.

245 1 0 $a Amazing Americans : $b Rosa Parks / $c Kristin Kemp, M.A.E.

246 3 0 $a Rosa Parks

490 1 $a Amazing Americans

830 0 $a Amazing Americans (Teacher Created Materials, Inc.)

In bibliographic records the series title, in the form it has on the resource, is recorded in MARC field 490 (see appendix D for more information). If the code of the first indicator of the 490 field is "1," then the series title, in its preferred form, is recorded in MARC field 830.

Some works that are published again and again, for example classic works of literature, have uniform titles. Usually the uniform title has two parts: the author's name, and the title of the work. Here is the authority record from the national authority file for the novel *Things Fall Apart*, by Chinua Achebe:

100 1 $a Achebe, Chinua. $t Things fall apart

670    $a Wikipedia, July 22, 2013 $b (Things Fall Apart is an English-language novel by Nigerian author Chinua Achebe published in 1958. It is seen as the archetypal modern African novel in English, and one of the first African novels written in English to receive global critical acclaim; was followed by a sequel, No Longer at Ease (1960), originally written as the second part of a larger work together with Things Fall Apart)

Having all works created by an author entered under the author's name is convenient because it means all of the author's works are indexed together. For example:

Achebe, Chinua
$t African trilogy
$t Anthills of the savannah.
$t Girls at war and other stories
$t Things fall apart

Like the uniform title for a work of literature, the uniform title of a work of classical music is given in two parts: the name of the composer, and information to identify the work. Because most classical music works do not have titles, but instead have numbers and information about the instrument or instruments the music is written for, that information becomes part of the uniform title. Here is the uniform title for Beethoven's ninth symphony:

100 1 $a Beethoven, Ludwig van, $d 1770-1827. $t Symphonies, $n no. 9, op. 125, $r D minor

Having musical works entered under the composer's name is helpful for library users who are looking for other works by the same composer. For example:

Beethoven, Ludwig van, $d 1770-1827.
$t Symphonies, $n no. 1, op. 21, $r C major
$t Symphonies, $n no. 2, op. 36, $r D major
$t Symphonies, $n no. 3, op. 55, $r E ♭ major
$t Symphonies, $n no. 4, op. 60, $r B ♭ major
$t Symphonies, $n no. 5, op. 67, $r C minor

Some uniform titles do not include an author, for example:

130 0 $a Bible

SUBJECT HEADINGS

All of the preferred headings discussed so far (names and titles) are constructed according to a content standard (usually AACR2 or RDA). Topical and geographical subject headings are not constructed this way, but rather come from a list of preferred subject terms, such as the *Sears List of Subject Headings* or the *Library of Congress Subject Headings*. Authority records for *Library of Congress Subject Headings* (LCSH) are discussed in this section: first, topical subject authority records, then geographical subject authority records.

Topical Subject Headings

The following is a topical subject authority record from the LCSH national authority file for clay animation films.

150	$a Clay animation films
450	$a Clay-mation films
450	$a Claymation films
450	$a Sculptmation films
550	$a Stop-motion animation films $w g
670	$a Work cat: Augusta makes herself beautiful, 1986.
670	$a World of animation, 1979: $b p. 25-28 (three-dimensional animation includes clay figures, puppets, cutouts ... ; discusses clay animation as part of puppet animation)
670	$a LC database, April 29, 1987 $b (clay animation; claymation)
670	$a Films by genre, 1993: $b (Clay animation, Claymation see Animated film: object animation films) p. 15 (when using clay, the terms Claymation and sculptmation are sometimes used for clay animation)
670	$a Wikipedia, Jan. 20, 2010 $b (Stop-motion animation using clay is described as clay animation or clay-mation)

The preferred subject term is given in the 150 field, while variant terms are given in 450 fields ("See" references). The term in the 550 field is a related term (a "See also" reference). The coding in the 550 field, subfield w, indicates the term in this field is a broader subject term than the term in the 100 field. Topical subject terms are recorded in 650 fields; here the preferred and variant terms are recorded in -50 fields—another instance of "rhyming" in MARC (see appendix D for more information).

Geographical Subject Headings

This is the geographical subject authority record from the national authority file for Dalarna, a province of Sweden:

034	$d E0140400 $e E0140400 $f N0610100 $g N061010 $g geonames
151	$a Dalarna (Sweden)
451	$a Dalecarlia (Sweden)
670	$a GeoNames [algorithmically matched] $b region; 61°01'00"N 014°04'00"E
781	$z Sweden $z Dalarna

The 151 field gives the preferred form of the name, while the 451 field contains a variant form of the name. The 034 and 670 fields reference GeoNames (www.geonames.org), an authoritative online database of place names, and give the geographical coordinates for Dalarna. The 670 field $b has "region," a term for the kind of geographical place Dalarna is. The 781 field gives the form to be used when adding this place name to a topical subject heading: the broader geographical heading "Sweden" would be given first, then "Dalarna." For example, to add the geographic location for Dalarna to the topical subject term "Agriculture," the name of the country, Sweden, is added between the subject term and the place name "Dalarna": Agriculture—Sweden—Dalarna.

Ways of Performing Authority Control

Authority control is practiced when catalogers choose authorized terms to add to bibliographic records, when they maintain a library's local authority file, when they perform post-cataloging cleanup, and when they contribute authority records to the national authority file. Because contributing authority records to the national authority file requires very specialized training, it will not be discussed in this book.

AUTHORITY CONTROL WHEN CATALOGING

When catalogers create or copy bibliographic records they perform a kind of authority control. They do this by researching and choosing the authorized forms of names, titles, subjects, and place names to include in bibliographic records.

For example, cataloger Tiffany Chavez is cataloging a book about the Rio Grande River written by John McPhee. She wants to use the authorized form of the author's name, so she looks up "McPhee, John" in OCLC's authority file. She finds seven names listed. She rules out the first name, "McPhee, John, 1796-1867," since this book was first published in 2013. Then she looks at the record for the second name, "McPhee, John, 1931-," and sees that this person has written books called *A Sense of Where You Are*, *The Pine Barrens*, and *Outcroppings*. Tiffany thinks this might be the same person as the author of the book she is cataloging, but she decides to look further before making a final decision. She sees that the book she is cataloging has "by the author of *The Pine Barrens*" listed in a blurb on the dust jacket. She now feels confident that she has found the appropriate authorized name, so she records "McPhee, John, 1931-" in the 100 field of the MARC record.

Next, Tiffany looks for an authorized heading for the Rio Grande River. She looks up "Rio Grande River" as a place name in OCLC's authority file and is referred to the authorized form: "Rio Grande (Colo.-Mexico and Tex.)." She records this heading in a 651 field.

The care taken by catalogers like Tiffany to ensure they are using the correct authorized headings goes a long way towards keeping a library's catalog useful for patrons. However, mistakes do happen, and that is where post-cataloging cleanup comes in.

POST-CATALOGING CLEANUP

A very important method of practicing authority control is post-cataloging cleanup. If a cataloger adds an unauthorized form of a heading to a bibliographic record, or assigns a heading for which there is no matching record in the local authority file, this can be discovered and addressed in a process called post-cataloging cleanup. This involves regularly running and processing reports (usually called "authority reports") that retrieve recently added headings that have no match in the local authority file.

Running Authority Reports

The frequency with which authority reports are run depends on the size of the library. At a large library, a report should probably be run every weekday.

At a smaller library, once per week or even less frequently may be adequate. The important thing is to run and process the reports regularly. Authority reports are run on a library's catalog, usually using the ILS's reporting function. The report is constructed to retrieve any entries in MARC fields subject to authority control that were added during a specific time period, and have no match in the authority file. The time period specified is usually the period since the previous report was run.

Processing Authority Reports

Once the report has been run, a cataloger must carefully investigate the results and determine if changes need to be made to the library's authority file, certain bibliographic records, or both. Changes may be made one by one or in a batch process. Following is a brief guide to some typical report findings and how to deal with them:

There are typographical errors. A cataloger may have added a bibliographic record with a heading that has a misspelling or typographical error. This will show up in the authority report because it has no exact match in the library's authority file. The solution is to correct the misspelled heading in the bibliographic record to match the authorized form of the heading.

Heading is authorized, but there is no record for it in the local authority file. If a cataloger adds a heading for which there is an authority record in the national authority file, but not in the local authority file, it will turn up in the authority report. The cataloger processing the report should search the national authority file for a record for that heading. If one is found, it is added to the local authority file.

Heading has been updated in the national authority file, but not in the local authority file. Headings, particularly headings for personal names, may be updated in the national authority file. This usually happens when a person dies and a death date is added to the record for his or her name. The appearance of the changed heading in the authority report is a prompt for the cataloger processing the report to update the heading in the local authority file. This is done by copying the updated record from the national authority file and using it to replace the old record in the local authority file. In addition to changing the record in the authority file, each biblio-

graphic record with the old form of the heading must be changed
to the updated form. This can be done one heading at a time or as
a batch, depending on the availability of software for making batch
changes.

*There is no authority record for a heading in the local authority file or in
the national authority file.*

- *Name and title headings*

  Not every name and title has an authorized form, so this
  is not necessarily a problem. The cataloger processing the
  report should confirm the absence of an authority record by
  conducting a thorough search of the national authority file.

- *Subject headings*

  On the other hand, every subject heading should be valid.
  Checking this can become complicated, because subject
  terms may be subdivided (i.e., they can be made more
  specific with added subheadings), and there will not be an
  authority record for every possible combination of subject
  terms and subheadings.

  In this case, the authority cataloger must validate the
  heading by checking that every heading and subheading
  has an authority record, that each may be used in the way it
  appears in the heading, and that the main subject heading
  and subheadings are in the correct order.

  For example, the subject heading: "Papermaking—
  Congresses—France" shows up in an authority report
  because there is no authority record for that exact
  combination of topical term and subheadings. Here is how
  the cataloger processing the report proceeds:

  - She looks at the bibliographic record in which the
    subject heading appears and sees the record represents
    a collection of conference papers about papermaking in
    France.
  - She looks up the authority record for "Papermaking"
    and sees that this is an authorized topical subject term.

- o She then looks at the authority record for "Congresses" and sees that this is an authorized "form" subheading (a subheading that describes what the resource *is*, as opposed to what it is *about*) that may be added to any topical term for a work consisting of publications from a conference about that topic.

- o She looks up "France," and sees that it is an authorized geographical subject heading. So far, so good.

- o She now has some questions about the order of the subheadings, so she looks closer at the authority records for "Papermaking," "Congresses," and "France." She sees that it is permissible for "Papermaking" to have a geographical subheading added after it, but this isn't true for "Congresses." This is a problem, since her heading is "Papermaking—Congresses—France."

- o Finally, she consults the Library of Congress's *Subject Headings Manual*. She sees that a typical order of subheadings is [Topical heading]—[Geographical heading]. She decides to change the order of the headings to: "Papermaking—France—Congresses."

Subject heading is from a controlled vocabulary not in use at your library. The coding of the second indicator of a 6XX field defines the controlled vocabulary from which a subject term is taken. For example, *Library of Congress Subject Headings* have a 6XX second indicator of "0," *Medical Subject Headings* have a 6XX second indicator of "2," and *Répertoire de vedettes-matière*, a set of French language terms, have a 6XX second indicator of "6." If a report turns up headings from a vocabulary that is not used at your library, the fields containing those headings may simply be deleted, as long as there are appropriate subject headings from the controlled vocabulary that is used at the library.

Subject term recorded in the wrong 6XX field. Different 6XX MARC fields contain different kinds of subject headings. 600 fields contain personal names as subject headings; 610 fields contain corporate body names as subject headings; and so on. Sometimes a cataloger records a subject heading in the wrong MARC field. For example, she may enter a geographical subject heading in a 650 field instead of a 651 field. Fortunately, this kind of error shows up in an authority report and can be corrected. The cataloger processing the report can usually just change the MARC tag to the correct one. (Of course, the heading should be checked to be sure it is authorized.)

Naturally, other situations may arise besides those shown above. However, all it takes to solve authority problems is time, a little effort, and some knowledge of how authority records work.

KEEPING UP WITH THE NATIONAL AUTHORITY FILE

The national authority file is always changing. New personal name, corporate name, and series title authority records are constantly being added; subject headings change; and personal name records are updated (e.g., when people die, the date of death is added). Because one of the goals of authority control is to keep a library's local authority file in harmony with the national authority file, catalogers need a strategy to keep up with all these changes. The following discussion reviews some of the ways the national authority file can change, and then address ways to incorporate the changes into the local authority file.

One of the most common changes to the national authority file is when personal name authority records change. For example, when the sitar player Ravi Shankar died in 2012, the preferred form in the authority record for his name in the national authority file was changed from "Shankar, Ravi, 1920-" to "Shankar, Ravi, 1920-2012." Another way national authority files change is by the addition of new authority records. Personal name authority records are the most frequently added, but new title, topical subject, and geographical records are also added from time to time.

Sometimes authority records become obsolete. When the Republic of Zaire changed its name to the Democratic Republic of Congo in 1997, the record for Zaire in the national authority file was changed. A note was added: "This heading is not valid for use as a subject. Works about this place are entered under Congo (Democratic Republic)." A new authority record was created for Congo (Democratic Republic). Authority catalogers had to update the authority record for Zaire in their local authority files, and add the new authority record for Congo (Democratic Republic). They also had to change every occurrence of the heading "Zaire" in bibliographic records to "Congo (Democratic Republic)."

So how do authority catalogers keep up with the changes to the national authority file? It depends on which kind of authority records is involved. There are two basic kinds: name and title authority records, and subject authority records. Keeping up with name and title authority records is relatively easy, because a local authority file only needs to have those personal name, corporate name, and uniform title authority records that support headings in the local catalog. For example, if the authority record changes for a series title, and your library doesn't own any of the parts of the series, you don't need to bother with it.

Topical and subject authority records are another matter. Fortunately, changes and additions to the list of subject headings don't happen very often. For *Library of Congress Subject Headings*, catalogers can find out about changes by checking the monthly list of changed headings, which can be accessed at www.loc.gov/aba/cataloging/subject/weeklylists. *Sears List of Subject Headings* is published by H. W. Wilson, and updated every few years in a new edition.

When headings in bibliographic records need to be changed in response to a change in the authority file, they can be changed one by one, or in a batch process using software built into the ILS. Third-party software, some of it free, is also available to work with ILSs to perform mass heading changes. The user e-mail list for a library's particular ILS is a good place to find out about this kind of software.

OUTSOURCING AUTHORITY WORK

Because post-cataloging cleanup and keeping the local authority file current is time- and staff-intensive, some librarians choose to outsource these parts of authority work. Authority control vendors can process ongoing updates and cleanup. They can also perform retrospective authority control for an entire library catalog. This is especially useful when authority work has not been done before, or has not been done for a long time. Contracting with a vendor may be a good choice for technical services departments without adequate staff or expertise to devote to performing full authority control locally. Keep in mind that it is possible to outsource some authority work while still doing some in-house. For example, a librarian may choose to outsource the authority work for a library's main collection, but create authority records in-house for a special collection of materials of local interest.

Catalog Maintenance

Catalog maintenance (sometimes called database maintenance) is usually discussed with authority control because it involves some similar processes: locating and correcting errors and updating records, often in a batch process. The most common catalog maintenance activities follow.

Location Changes

When a library resource is moved from one part of the library to another, the location in the catalog record needs to change, too, so patrons and library staff can still find the resource.

Withdrawals

When library resources are withdrawn or go missing, their records need to be removed from the catalog. Care should be taken when deleting records from the catalog—sometimes useful information such as purchase order or circulation history is attached to a catalog record and will be lost if the record is deleted. An alternative to deletion is suppressing the record so it is still visible on the "back side" of the catalog, but hidden from the user in the OPAC.

Reinstatements

Sometimes library materials that go missing are found or replaced. In these cases, if the record was suppressed when the material was withdrawn, it can be "unsuppressed," and made visible again in the OPAC.

Correcting Errors

Many different kinds of errors can crop up in a library catalog. Most require some kind of active investigation in order to be discovered.

TYPOGRAPHICAL ERRORS (TYPOS) AND MISSPELLINGS

Many catalogers subscribe to lists and blogs devoted to common typos in library catalogs and other databases. Keyword searches for typos will turn up errors to be corrected. For example, instances of the typo "actino" (for the word "action") may be found by searching the catalog using the word "actino." Caution should be exercised, because a word may be a typo in some circumstances, but not in others. For example, "meting" could be a misspelling of the word "meeting," or it could be the correctly spelled form of the English word that means distributing by measure. It's a good idea never to do mass changes to correct typographical errors or misspellings.

REMOVING OR CORRECTING DEAD HYPERLINKS

Sometimes a hyperlink in a catalog record may stop working. This bugaboo is particularly common in older records not using persistent URLs (PURLs). There are different reasons why a hyperlink may fail: the webpage the link points to may no longer exist; the page may have moved to a different domain; or the site may have been reorganized, resulting in a changed Uniform Resource Locator (URL). Dead links can be detected by running a report that is built into a library's ILS. Another way is to export all the URLs to a file, then run the file through a link-checking software program. Correcting (or deleting) the broken links must be done one by one, manually, and usually requires investigative work to locate a newer, active link. If you find you no longer have access to resources you have paid for, refer this issue to the acquisitions unit, especially to the people who work with your ERMS. As with running and processing authority reports, link checking is best done on a regular basis.

Many other kinds of catalog changes may fall under the bailiwick of catalog maintenance. With diligence and knowledge of the workings of the catalog you can resolve just about any problem.

Trends and Issues in Authority Control and Catalog Maintenance

Some authority control librarians are currently wrestling with an issue that began when the national authority was converted to be RDA-compliant in early 2013. This created a fair amount of work for authority control catalogers. RDA has not been implemented at all libraries; at those where it has been only partially implemented, a local authority file may include both AACR2- and RDA-compliant records. This can create problems in the index display of authorized headings, "See" references, and "See also" references.

A trend in authority control principles is the development of *Functional Requirements for Authority Data* (FRAD), a conceptual model for authority data. FRAD was developed to apply the *Functional Requirements for Bibliographic Records* (FRBR) principles to authority work. FRAD defines user tasks as well as functions of the authority file. For more information, visit the FRAD website at www.ifla.org/publications/functional-requirements-for -authority-data.

Another authority control trend is the development of the Virtual International Authority File (VIAF). This is a service that began as a test project to link name authority records across languages and international boundaries. VIAF groups authority records from different national authority files into cluster records for each unique name. As of this writing, VIAF is not of much use to catalogers in their everyday work, but it promises to become more important in the future. Someday, instead of typing or copying the preferred form of a person's name into a bibliographic record, a cataloger might simply provide a link to the VIAF record for that name. The local ILS would know to display only the form of the name that is in the language of the local catalog. More information about VIAF can be found at http://viaf.org.

Faceted Application of Subject Terminology (FAST) is an OCLC research project. Its goal is to modify the *Library of Congress Subject Headings* and create a more simplified way of creating strings of subject terms. OCLC has added FAST subject headings to many of the bibliographic records in its database. More information about FAST is available at www.oclc.org/research/ themes/data-science/fast.html.

Final Thoughts

Although most cataloging is concerned with creating or copying individual bibliographic records, authority control and catalog maintenance are concerned with the library catalog as a whole. Authority control creates invisible links between records that allow patrons and staff to retrieve every record with the same author, series title, or subject with one search. With authority control, similar names, titles, and subject terms are differentiated from each other, avoiding confusion and aiding precise searching. Likewise, a clean database—one free of misspellings, typographical errors, and broken links—is much more useful than one filled with errors. Authority control is time-consuming, but because it contributes so much to the usefulness of the catalog, most agree it is worthwhile.

Resources

Block, Rick. "Authority Control: What It Is, and Why It Matters." 1999. www.columbia.edu/cu/libraries/inside/units/bibcontrol/osmc.

FAST (Faceted Application of Subject Terminology). www.oclc.org/research/themes/data-science/fast.html.

IFLA Working Group on Functional Requirements and Numbering of Authority Records. *Functional Requirements for Authority Data.* www.ifla.org/publications/functional-requirements-for-authority-data.

MARC 21 Format for Authority Data. www.loc.gov/marc/authority.

Maxwell, Robert L. *Maxwell's Guide to Authority Work.* Chicago: American Library Association, 2002.

Subject Headings Manual. Washington, DC: Library of Congress, Policy and Support Office, 2008.

Understanding MARC Authority Records: Machine-Readable Cataloging. 2004. www.loc.gov/marc/uma.

VIAF: Virtual International Authority File. http://viaf.org.

Collection Management

Collection management is a general term that encompasses several different activities. Ideally, it involves staff from many different parts of the library, including cataloging, physical processing, systems, and public services. In some cases, it can also include planning the management of physical locations, such as shifting collections to allow for growth, or moving an entire collection to a different part of the library. (This facet is most often associated with access services or public services rather than technical services.) Some collection management activities that can be the purview of technical services are discussed in this chapter. The activities related to cataloging, such as database maintenance and withdrawing materials from the catalog, are discussed in chapter 7.

This chapter will cover:

- Reviewing gift materials
- Repairing damaged materials
- Deselection (weeding)
- Replacement of lost and missing items
- Disaster preparedness
- Trends and issues in collection management

Before You Begin

Before you begin working in collection management, you will need to familiarize yourself with your library's policies on gifts, material repair, deselection, lost materials, replacement materials, stack maintenance, disaster preparedness, and periodical retention. Some of these will be discussed here, but others, such as stacks maintenance, are not under the purview of technical services, and will only be touched on briefly.

You will also need to know about the attitudes of the staff involved with collection management. There are some parts of collection maintenance, such as deselection, which can be both politically and emotionally charged for library staff and the patron base of your institution. Understanding the attitudes of the involved staff is critical to develop a smoothly functioning collection maintenance program.

Specialized Terms

Deselection/weeding—The process of examining the materials in a collection to determine which ones should remain in the collection and which should be removed.

Discards—Materials removed from a collection.

Dust jacket—The folded paper covering over most hardback books.

Gifts—Donations to the library. There are usually two types:

Cash—Money, or other negotiable asset, given to the library to support the library's programs.

In-kind—Materials given to the library with the intention that they be added to the collection.

Mylar cover—These are clear covers that are folded around dust jackets on hardback books and then attached using either glue or tape.

Parts of a book—Figure 8.1 illustrates the following parts of a book to which this chapter will refer:

Endpapers—The papers inside the front and back covers along with the page facing them.

Gutter—Where two facing pages meet when a book is open.

Hinge—Inside the front and back covers, where the text block is connected to the covers.

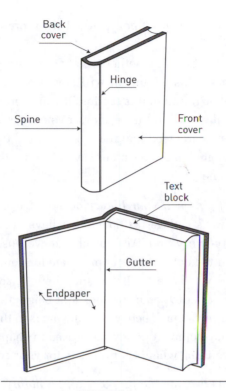

FIGURE 8.1
Parts of a book

Signature—Two or more sheets of paper folded together in preparation for binding.

Spine—The outside bound edge of the book

Text block—The pages of a book

Tip (tipping) in—The process of gluing in replacement pages by the tips of the pages.

Withdrawals—The process of removing discards from the catalog.

Reviewing Gift Materials

This section looks at in-kind donations, that is, books, DVDs, and other materials that are given to the library. Gifts can be a great way to expand your library's collection. However, if not handled with forethought and care they can also be a nightmare.

The first thing to check is whether or not your library has a gift and donation policy in place. This document will have the answers to many of the questions that will be raised in this section. If your library doesn't have a policy, then check with your funding agency. If you are in a public or academic library, it is almost guaranteed that there is a gift and donation policy, but it may need to be updated. If there isn't one, you can use the questions outlined below to develop one.

What kinds of gifts will your library accept? Large runs of periodicals? Uncle Fred's college textbooks that have been in his attic for the past forty-five years? Well-loved and well-used children's books? You need to know what is appropriate for your collection and what resources you have for processing them. If someone calls about a donation, offer to come and look at it before they bring it over. This will give you a much better idea of what is in the donation. Your collection development policy (discussed in chapter 1), will be helpful for determining what is appropriate for your collection.

When do books become the property of the library? When they come in the door, or when they are accepted for the collection? The answer to this question makes a big difference when you are trying to dispose of materials you don't want. For example, at some university libraries, gifts become the property of the university as soon as they come in the door. This means that anything the library doesn't want to keep must go through the same disposal procedure as other university property. This procedure is much more onerous than simply throwing unwanted books away or finding them a home at another institution.

What condition are the materials in? If at all possible, open boxes of donations outside of your building. Insect infestations, as well as mold and mildew infiltrations, have been caused by donations in poor condition being brought into the building before they were checked for problems.

Can you turn down in-kind donations? If a donation doesn't look like it will be worth processing, can you thank the donor and suggest other

Acknowledging In-Kind Donations

Every library should acknowledge donations whenever possible. The gift policy should prescribe the language of the acknowledgment so it is consistent with all legalities required by your funding agency. (Note that the following only applies to in-kind donations.) At a minimum, an acknowledgment letter should include that date of the donation, a description of it (i.e., number of volumes, format, fiction versus nonfiction), and a disclaimer (usually boilerplate that has been vetted by the institution's lawyers) that states that the library reserves the right to decide whether or not a donation will be added to the collection, and that it may be disposed of as the library sees fit.

Do not include an estimated value of the donation in the acknowledgment, even if donors request this information for tax purposes. Unless you are a duly licensed appraiser, you are not qualified to tell the donor the fair market value of the donation. If you do, and the Internal Revenue Service or your state revenue department later audits a donor and decides the donation was overvalued, you have opened your institution up for prosecution, and possibly placed your non-profit standing in jeopardy.

Be careful about accepting gifts with conditions attached. If a donor wants specific guarantees regarding a donation, refer her to the head of your library.

libraries or places that will get more use out of it? Hospitals, nursing homes, and other long-term care facilities often accept materials.

When small donations are just dropped off at the library, either by patrons or anonymously, they can be treated on a case-by-case basis. Training frontline circulation staff to evaluate can be helpful for keeping this under control.

Please see the sidebar for additional information on acknowledging donations.

Repairing Damaged Materials

This activity is often included in technical services because the equipment and supplies used are closely related those used in physical processing. Both involve physically handling the items and using materials like tape, glue, and boxes to ensure the materials will remain usable as long as possible under regular library conditions. When you are working with new materials, this can include reinforcing the covers of paperbacks with tape, or reinforcing the spines of books with glue and additional stiffeners. When repairing damaged books, the same materials are often used to reinforce the same parts of the books. However, repair may be more involved. It can include tipping in (gluing in loose or replacement pages), repairing the front and back hinges of an item where the text block is pulling out, or a myriad of other major and minor repairs.

Deciding When to Repair

Before you begin repairing an item, there are some questions you need to ask. First, is there a policy for when to repair an item and when to replace it? If there isn't, you may need to develop one. If there isn't a policy, you should ask the following questions when evaluating an item for repair:

> *Should the item be deselected?* Many materials just aren't worth keeping. For more information on this, see the section on deselection later in this chapter.

> *Is the item still available for purchase?* If it is more cost efficient to purchase a new copy, that would be the route to take.

> *How extensive are the needed repairs?* Often, by the time an item gets to the repairing stage there is so much damage that it can't be saved.

These are just a few of the questions that go into deciding whether or not to repair an item. As hard as it is, you must be brutally honest about whether or not you should fix any item.

Once you have determined that the item in hand needs to be repaired, do you have the expertise to repair it in house, or do you need to send it to a professional conservator? Professional conservators are expensive, but if you are dealing with a one-of-a-kind item that is important to, for example, your local history collection, they are well worth the expense.

Types of Repairs

Because there are entire books and courses on how to repair books, this will not be discussed in detail, but rather give examples of what are usually considered "basic" repairs versus repairs that should either be sent out to a specialist or trigger replacement if possible.

Basic repairs include:

- reinforcing the edges of the covers, hinges, or spine
- repairing small rips in pages
- tipping in a few pages when the adjoining pages are still tight
- building boxes for materials that are too fragile to repair
- drying books (if pages are not stuck together)
- erasing pencil marks

More advanced repairs (which may require outsourcing or replacing the item) include:

- complete rebinding
- repairing or replacing badly damaged spines
- reopening books that have been wet and the pages are stuck together
- tipping in pages when multiple pages are loose
- cleaning crayon or ink marks
- damage from urine
- mold, mildew, and insect infestations

Special Handling

In most cases, damaged materials don't need special handling beyond what would be done for fragile items. However, in the case of wet, moldy, mildewed, or insect-infested materials, there are some special handling requirements for the protection of your staff and your collections.

For wet materials, if you aren't able to start drying them immediately, wrap them in plastic and put them in the freezer. This will slow down any additional damage and limit the growth of mold and mildew. Don't forget to let them thaw thoroughly before beginning to work on conserving them.

For moldy, mildewed, and insect-infested materials, immediately put them into a zip-top bag. Mold, mildew, and insects can infest a library collection very easily, so you will need to bag affected materials as soon as you can. Clear bags are preferred, because you can see any problems without opening them.

Deselection (Weeding)

The process of deselecting, or weeding, library materials involves several decisions, most of which are made before the materials reach technical services. However, once the decision to weed has been made, technical services will be involved in parts of the process. Some, like appropriately editing various catalog records, fall under catalog maintenance (see chapter 7 for more information). Physical processing may be responsible for marking materials as withdrawn and removing property stamps. Acquisitions may be responsible for developing lists of materials that should be ordered to fill in gaps created by weeding older materials.

Weeding should be done on a regular basis, but it is often at the bottom of the list when it comes to priorities. Although technical services staff are rarely on the front line of most weeding projects, their assistance can be critical for success. Many times, it is the technical services staff who have the expertise to run various collection reports from the ILS. These reports include a wealth of information to aid a weeding project. This information includes:

- average age of collection by classification range
- circulation statistics by classification range
- collection size
- collection turnover (average circulation)

All this information helps the staff doing the actual weeding to know which parts of the collection need to be addressed first due to either lack of, or heavy, use.

Replacement of Lost and Missing Items

It is a fact of life that materials will be lost or go missing, and need to be replaced. Sometimes, for example, when a patron loses an item, you may be able to collect the money needed to replace it. When materials just disappear, you will have to pay for the replacement out of your budget. It is prudent to run a lost and missing report from your ILS on a regular basis. How often the report is run will vary depending on the size of the library, how busy it is, and the historical practices of the library.

After you run the lost and missing report, there are some decisions you and your selectors need to make.

> *Which titles need to be replaced?* If you have other copies, or a title is old or superseded, you probably don't need to replace it.

> *Which titles can be replaced?* Some items may be out of print or otherwise unavailable.

> *How much can you afford to replace?* Replacing the entire list will probably cost more than you have budgeted, so you will need to prioritize which titles you will replace and in what order.

After you have made these decisions, the titles can be ordered by the acquisitions unit. However, note that the orders are for replacements, so that catalogers know that there is already a record in the ILS for that item, and they will only need to add a new copy.

Titles that will not be replaced need to be passed on to catalog maintenance to have the copy holdings record removed or suppressed from the system, and, if necessary, the bibliographic record removed or suppressed as well.

Disaster Preparedness

Disaster can strike any library at any time. Fires and floods have many causes, and run the gamut from minor irritations to substantial loss. Having a disaster preparedness plan in place and basic supplies on hand can mean the difference between one or the other.

The role technical services plays in the disaster plan will vary by institution. Often, technical services becomes the repository for disaster response supplies since it is out of the public eye, yet accessible by most staff. The physical processing department's knowledge of mending, conservation, and preservation can be critical to recovery efforts. It is important to study and regularly review the disaster plan to maintain its accuracy. At a minimum,

technical services staff should know how to use any disaster response supplies housed in their area.

It is also helpful to include a notebook of emergency resources with your
disaster response supplies. This can include outside contractors you might
need to call in case of disaster. Having information on, for example, the clos-
est source of industrial freezers (in case a large part of the collection is water
damaged), and contact information for your insurance company in one place
that's easy to find can be critical during a power failure.

Disaster response supplies should be kept in a centralized location in
each library building. They will also need to be inventoried on a regular
basis. Some supplies have limited shelf lives and will need to be updated regularly. Some materials might have been "borrowed" for other projects around
the library—the plastic sheeting used to protect bookshelves from water leaks
is especially tempting to paint crews who need drop cloths and librarians
who need to protect the floor from messy craft projects.

Trends and Issues in Collection Management

There are several issues facing collection management in the next five to ten
years. First among these is the ongoing space crisis that many, if not most,
libraries have. Due to the economic downturn during the first decade of the
2000s, the amount of money available for replacing, upgrading, and renovat-
ing buildings has been drastically cut. Libraries that have not been proactive
in managing their collections face a growing shortage of space as their physical collections grow.

The shift towards electronic resources is also a trend that bears watching
from the viewpoint of collection management. Although it helps to amelio-
rate some of the space issues, it brings with it a whole host of other issues
that need to be addressed, including how to weed, archive, preserve, and
access them.

Resources

Cassell, Kay Ann. "Handling Gift Books in Libraries: A View from the US." *New Library World* 106 (May 2005): 450–453.

Dartmouth College Preservation Services, *A Simple Book Repair Manual.* Hanover, NH: Board of the Trustees of Dartmouth College, 1996.

Kahn, Miriam. *Disaster Response and Planning for Libraries.* 2nd ed. Chicago: American Library Association, 2003.

Larson, J. *CREW: A Weeding Method for Modern Libraries.* Austin, TX: Texas State Library and Archives Commission, 2012.

Wellheiser, Johanna G., and Jude Scott. *An Ounce of Prevention: Integrated Disaster Planning for Archives, Libraries, and Record Centers.* 2nd ed. Lanham, MD: Scarecrow Press, 2002.

Content Standards

Content standards provide detailed guidance about which pieces of infor-mation to include in a bibliographic record, how to record that information, and how to construct access points. (Access points are specific pieces of information, including author, title, and subject, which can be searched in the catalog.) This process is called descriptive cataloging. Until recently, the most commonly used content standard in most libraries was *Anglo-American Cataloguing Rules,* Second Edition, Revised (AACR2R). The first version of this standard, *Anglo-American Cataloguing Rules* (AACR), was developed cooperatively in 1967 by various library associations, including the American Library Association and the Library Association (Britain). In 1974, a complete revision of AACR was undertaken. This resulted in *Anglo-American Cataloguing Rules,* Second Edition (AACR2). Further revisions were made in 1988, 1998, and 2002. As of 2005, it is no longer being revised and focus has shifted to a new content standard, *Resource Description and Access* (RDA).

Published in 2010, RDA was developed by a wider group of libraries and library associations than AACR2 and was subsequently adopted at many libraries. RDA was developed to address the changes in libraries and technology that occurred after AACR2 was written. Among these changes are: the shift from libraries collecting mostly printed books to collecting more audiovisual and electronic resources; the automation of most library catalogs; the advent of the World Wide Web; and the development of *Functional Requirements for Bibliographic Records* (FRBR), a new "conceptual model of the bibliographic universe." FRBR is based on the entity-relationship model, in which a database is made up of *entities* (each of which has defined *attributes*), and *relationships* between entities. For more information about FRBR, see the list of resources at the end of this appendix.

Although a detailed treatment of the differences between AACR2 and RDA will not be given here, those that are the most noticeable in catalog records are reviewed.

> RDA incorporates the FRBR model, which means it defines different kinds of bibliographic entities, their attributes, and the relationships between entities. Relationships appear in RDA catalog records as *relator codes*. For example, when recording the author of *The Adventures of Tom Sawyer*, the entry would read: "Twain, Mark, 1835-1910. author." This indicates Mark Twain has the relationship *author* to the title *The Adventures of Tom Sawyer*. RDA defines many other bibliographic relationships. If this is starting to sound very complicated, please remember it isn't necessary to have a deep understanding of the concepts behind RDA in order to use it.

> In AACR2 cataloging, a General Material Designation (GMD), a piece of information indicating the nature of a resource, is added in brackets after the title in records for certain non-book resources. For example, the record for an e-book accessed online would read: "*The girl who kicked the hornet's nest* [electronic resource]."

> The GMD is not used in RDA cataloging. Instead, three *aspects* are recorded for every kind of resource: its *content* (the form of communication through which the content is expressed); its *medium* (the general type of device required to view, play, run, or otherwise access a resource); and its *carrier* (the resource's physical storage medium). In the case of the online e-book, its content would be recorded as "text," its medium as "computer," and its carrier as "online." These aspects are recorded in MARC fields 336, 337, and 338.

> AACR2 limits how many authors may be recorded in a catalog record to three. In RDA cataloging, there is no restriction on the number of authors that may be included in a record.

> AACR2 requires many words to be abbreviated. For example, "p." is recorded for "pages," "ill." for "illustrations," and "Dept." for "Department." Abbreviations were heavily used to save space on the old 3" x 5" catalog cards. RDA eliminates the use of almost all abbreviations.

AACR2 uses abbreviated Latin terms in certain situations. For example, if the place of publication is not known, the abbreviation "s.l.," for *sine loco* (without a location), is used. If the name of the publisher is not known, "s.n.," for *sine nomine* (without a name), is used. In order to make catalog records more understandable to library users, RDA replaces these Latin abbreviations with the English phrases "Place of publication not identified" and "Publisher not identified."

In practice, cataloging with RDA is quite similar to cataloging with AACR2. In addition, RDA was designed to be compatible with AACR2, so catalogers do not need to update older AACR2 records to RDA. Eventually, so many libraries will have adopted RDA that it will be difficult to find AACR2 records for copy cataloging, so it is wise for AACR2 catalogers to learn about RDA. RDA is available both in print and as an online, searchable electronic resource called the RDA Toolkit. AACR2 is no longer available in print; however, it is available through Cataloger's Desktop, a subscription-based, online compendium of cataloging tools. An abridged version, *The Concise AACR2*, is a very useful resource that is still available in print.

RESOURCES

Cataloger's Desktop. 2014. www.loc.gov/cds/products/product.php?product ID=162.

Gorman, Michael. *The Concise AACR2*. 4th ed. Chicago: American Library Association, 2004.

Hart, Amy. *The RDA Primer: A Guide for the Occasional Cataloger.* Santa Barbara: Linworth, 2010.

Maxwell, Robert L. *Maxwell's Handbook for AACR2*. 4th ed. Chicago: American Library Association, 2004.

———. *Maxwell's Handbook for RDA*. Chicago: American Library Association, 2013.

Tillett, Barbara. "What Is FRBR? A Conceptual Model for the Bibliographic Universe." 2004. www.loc.gov/cds/downloads/FRBR.PDF.

RDA: Resource Description and Access—2014 Revision. Chicago: American Library Association, 2014.

RDA Toolkit. www.rdatoolkit.org.

Classification Systems and Call Numbers

Classification systems divide the world of knowledge into broad classes, each of which is further subdivided into smaller and smaller divisions for more and more specific topics. Topics are represented by codes, which catalogers assign to library materials. Classification systems allows resources with similar topics to be located near each other, so that library users can discover materials by browsing the shelves or the online catalog. The most familiar classification systems in the United States are Dewey Decimal Classification (DDC), widely used in public and school libraries, and Library of Congress Classification (LCC), which is more common in academic libraries.

Catalogers add other pieces of information to the classification number to create a call number—a code that gives a resource a specific location on the shelf or in the library's catalog. The first piece of added information is a *Cutter number*, sometimes simply called a Cutter. A Cutter usually starts with first letter of the author's last name, followed by two or more numbers that represent the next letters of the last name. Cutters serve to order materials alphabetically on the shelf and in the catalog. The final piece of added information in a call number is the publication date of the resource.

Dewey Decimal Classification

Dewey Decimal Classification (DDC) is made up of ten broad subject classes:

- 000 Computer science, information and general works
- 100 Philosophy and psychology
- 200 Religion

300   Social sciences

400   Language

500   Science

600   Technology

700   Arts and recreation

800   Literature

900   History & geography

Each subject class is divided into ten divisions representing narrower topics, and each division is further divided into ten sections. The example will be a 2015 book by Carlos Marías about digital photography in Spain:

The DDC class 700–799 is for Arts and recreation.

The division 770–779 is for Photography

775 is the DDC number for Digital photography.

DDC includes tables that can be used to make a classification number even more specific in a process called *number-building*. Consult DDC's geography table to find a number to add to the basic class number to indicate that a resource's subject matter is specific to Spain. The geographical number for Spain is .946; therefore, that number is added to 775 to come up with a classification for digital photography in Spain.

The final classification number is 775.946.

Cutter numbers for Dewey call numbers are created using either a Cutter-Sanborn table (a set of books that give Cutter numbers for just about every possible combination of letters) or specialized software. OCLC provides a free software program for creating Dewey Cutters; for details, see the list of resources at the end of this appendix. When the first three letters of the author's last name are entered, the software produces the Cutter M323. With the Cutter number and date of publication added, the final call number for the book is:

775.946

M323

2015

Dewey Decimal Classification is laid out in detail in a four-volume book, currently in its twenty-third revision, or in a one-volume abridgement in its fifteenth edition. It is also available by subscription as WebDewey, an interactive electronic version.

Library of Congress Classification

Like DDC, Library of Congress Classification (LCC) is structured hierarchi-
cally. It is made up of twenty-one alphanumeric classes, each of which is further divided by topic. Here are the highest level classes of LCC:

A   General works

B   Philosophy, psychology, religion

C   Auxiliary sciences of history

D   History: general and Old World

E   History: America

F   History: United States Local

G   Geography, anthropology, recreation

H   Social sciences

J   Political science

K   Law

L   Education

M   Music

N   Fine arts

P   Language and literature

Q   Science

R   Medicine

S   Agriculture

T   Technology

U   Military science

V   Naval science

Z   Bibliography, library science

Each broad subject class is divided into smaller subject divisions. For example, when cataloging a 2014 book by Sherry Foster about endangered species in New Mexico, going to QL, the subdivision for zoology, will show this range:

QL81.5–QL84.7   Wildlife conservation, Rare animals, Endangered species, Wildlife refuges, Wildlife habitat improvement.

QL84.22 is a class number for specific states.

LCC uses Cutter numbers to divide topics by geographical location, so the Cutter number for New Mexico, .N6, is added. (Note that in LCC, call numbers can have more than one Cutter number.)

The Cutter number for the author is determined by consulting a special Library of Congress table. The Cutter for Foster is F67.

When the year of publication is added, the call number is complete:

QL
84.22
N6
F67
2014

A full version of Library of Congress Classification is available as a set of PDF files on the Library of Congress's website. It is also available by subscription in an interactive online electronic version called Classification Web. See the list of resources below for details.

RESOURCES

Cataloger's Desktop. 2014. www.loc.gov/cds/products/product.php?product ID=162.

Classification Web. 2015. https://classificationweb.net.

Dewey Cutter Program. 2015. https://oclc.org/support/services/dewey/program .en.html.

Dewey Decimal System—A Guide to Call Numbers. 2011. www.library.illinois .edu/ugl/about/dewey.html.

Dewey, Melvil. *Abridged Dewey Decimal Classification and Relative Index*. Dublin, OH: OCLC Online Computer Library Center, 2012.

Dewey, Melvil. *Dewey Decimal Classification and Relative Index*. Dublin, OH: OCLC Online Computer Library Center, 2011.

Library of Congress Classification PDF Files. 2015. www.loc.gov/aba/publica
     tions/FreeLCC/freelcc.html#About.
Library of Congress Classification Outline. www.loc.gov/catdir/cpso/lcco.
WebDewey. 2015. www.oclc.org/dewey/features.en.html#webdewey.

APPENDIX C

Subject Term Lists

*Subject term lists are sets of preferred words or phrases used to provide sub-*ject access to library resources. The most widely used subject term lists in the United States are *Sears Subject Headings* (Sears) and the *Library of Congress Subject Headings* (LCSH), both of which are designed for general use. There are also specialized subject term lists, for example, *Medical Subject Headings* (MeSH), and the National Agricultural Library's *Agricultural Thesaurus*. These subject term lists include more precise and technical terms that are designed for specialists.

In bibliographic records, subject terms are access points, meaning they may be searched in the catalog as phrases, not just as keywords. When catalogers consistently use the same subject term to describe resources about a particular topic, patrons are able to find all of the library's resources on that topic by using the subject term when they search the catalog. Subject access points are also called "subject headings."

Most subject term lists are set up to direct patrons to the preferred term for a subject if they search using a different term that has the same meaning. For example, in the *Library of Congress Subject Headings* (LCSH), the pre-ferred term for pigs is "Swine." If a patron at a library using LCSH searches for the subject term "Pigs," he will be directed to search under the term "Swine" instead. When he searches using the term "Swine," he will retrieve all the resources in that library that are about pigs.

Subheadings can be added to subject terms to make a heading more spe-cific. For example, for a book about knitting in Ireland between 1800 and 1899, a cataloger assigns the Library of Congress subject heading **Knitting**.

Then she adds a geographical subheading so she now has the subject string **Knitting—Ireland**.

Finally, she adds another subheading for the time period covered by the book. The final subject string is **Knitting—Ireland—19th century**.

Names of people, place names, names of organizations, book titles, and titles of musical works may all be used as subject terms in catalog records. For example, even though William Shakespeare is widely known as an author, a biography about Shakespeare would have his name as a subject entry, with a subheading indicating the resource is a biography: **Shakespeare, William, 1564-1616—Biography**. A book about his play *Hamlet* would have the subject heading: **Shakespeare, William, 1564-1616—Hamlet**.

Most library patrons use keywords to search the catalog, so you may be wondering why anyone bothers to include subject headings if people don't use them when searching. The reason is that subject terms are made up of searchable keywords, and without subject headings, some resources are unlikely to be found with keywords searches. For example, the book *Thunderstruck* by Erik Larson is a true story about Guglielmo Marconi, the inventor of the telegraph, and how his invention helped catch a murderer. The subject is not apparent from the title of the book. But because the record includes keyword searchable subject headings for *Marconi*, *inventors*, *telegraph*, *murder*, and *murderers*, a library user who entered the keywords "Marconi" and "murder" or "telegraph" and "murder" would retrieve the record for the book. Without the subject headings, patrons would not be able to find this book unless they knew the title or the name of the author.

Subject term lists help make shared cataloging possible because so many libraries use the same lists of subject terms. When a cataloger in Poughkeepsie contributes an original record to a bibliographic utility that has LCSH, a cataloger in Portland at a library that uses LCSH can import the record into her library's catalog without thinking twice about the subject headings.

RESOURCES

Library of Congress Authorities. 2015. http://authorities.loc.gov.

Library of Congress Subject Headings. 35th ed. Washington, DC: Library of Congress, 2013.

Sears List of Subject Headings. 21st ed. Ipswich, MA: H. W. Wilson, a division of EBSCO Information Services, 2014.

MARC Digital Format

A standard digital format allows catalog records to exist in digital form, have a coherent structure, and be displayed on computer screens. When different catalogers use the same digital standard, they can exchange electronic records with each other. The Machine-Readable Cataloging (MARC) digital standard was developed in the 1960s and is still widely used today. The most recent version of the MARC standard is MARC 21. Because it is a standard, it provides rules and guidelines for catalogers to follow. There are three types of MARC formats commonly used in library catalogs: MARC Bibliographic, which provides a format for bibliographic records; MARC Holdings, which provides a format for copy holdings records; and MARC Authority, which provides a format for authority records (see chapter 7).

All MARC records are made up of long strings of numbers and letters. They are difficult to view and edit in their "raw" form (see figure D.1), so most catalogers choose to work with MARC records in their library's cataloging module or other specialized software. These programs divide the string of characters into discrete fields, making the record much easier to view and edit. Because MARC is used in a computing environment, the characters (letters and numbers) in a MARC record use a standard character encoding scheme developed for computers. The first encoding standard used in MARC records, still in use today, is MARC-8. It was created for use with MARC and is not used outside libraries. In the 1990s, a multilingual character encoding standard, Unicode, was developed and widely adopted for many computer applications, including library catalogs. Unicode is very popular because it supports over 100,000 characters in many scripts, including Han Chinese,

Hebrew, and Arabic. A form of Unicode, UTF-8, was approved for use in MARC records in 1998. The character encoding standard in a MARC record is invisible in most English language records. So why discuss it here? The choice of character encoding standard becomes important when transferring a MARC record between systems, for example, when importing a record from a bibliographic utility. If the record is exported from the utility in MARC-8 format, but the ILS is expecting to import records in UTF-8 format, the ILS may not recognize the MARC-8 record. If this happens, you may need to check the settings for character encoding in your bibliographic utility's cataloging software and in your ILS (see figure D.1).

No matter what character coding standard is used, MARC records have two kinds of fields: *fixed fields* and *variable fields*. Fixed fields have a set length; that is, each can hold only a certain number of characters. Fixed fields don't display in the OPAC, but they do appear in the back side of the catalog. Even though they aren't visible to library patrons, they can be a mechanism for searching the catalog. For example, there is a MARC Bibliographic fixed field area where the language of a resource is given in a three-letter code. The code is for Portuguese is "por." If a user were searching for library resources in Portuguese, the library's catalog software would retrieve records with the code "por" in the fixed field for language (see figure D.2).

Variable fields are as long as they need to be to include their contents, and make up most of what a patron sees in the OPAC. Each variable field has three parts: a tag, indicators, and subfields. A *tag* is simply a three-digit number given to a MARC field to identify it. Every MARC variable field has two spaces for *indicators*, even though they are not required to be coded for every variable field. The codes for indicators differ depending on the field they are in. For example, the second indicator of the MARC Bibliographic subject term field 650 is coded to show which controlled vocabulary the subject term is from. The bulk of a variable field is made up of *subfields*. Each subfield has a code, usually a letter, and a symbol (a delimiter) that separates it from other subfields. The delimiter symbol is represented different ways, usually as either "‡" (double dagger) or "$" (dollar sign). For example, in the MARC 21 Bibliographic 245 field, the first subfield ($a) is where the first part of the title is recorded. The second subfield ($b) is where the rest of the title is recorded. The statement of responsibility (the author or authors) is recorded in the third subfield ($c) (see figure D.3).

02844cjm a2200565 a 450000100130000000030006000130050017000190070015000360
08004100051010001700092040000590010901900140016802400170018202400280019900
28002300022704200140025008200140026404900090027810000270028724500750031420
60003100038930000570042051100640047751801030054150000190064450000470066350
50650200710505036801362538001901730650001001749650001701757596500019017767
00002501795700002901820700002501849700002501874700002501899700003801924700
00350196270000230199770000350202070000250205570000210208071000340210170
10003502135710003202170710003402202710003002236994001202266-ocm79858629
-OCoLC-20130505025819.0-sd fsngnnmmneu-090409p20061956nyujznn fi   n eng
d- a 2009603377- aVVWbengcDLCdVVWdlBl- dVP@dBTCTAdBDXdGRPVEdOCLCO-
a150305215-1 a602517052383-7 a006025170523832gtin-14-02-aB0007423-02bVerve-
alccopycat-04a781.5 FIT- aIRUU-1 aFitzgerald, Ella.4prf-14aThe very best of the song
booksh[sound recording] /cElla Fitzgerald.- aNew York :bVerve,cp2006.- a2 sound
discs :bdigital ;-c4 3/4 in. +e1 pamphlet.-0 aElla Fitzgerald, vocals ; with various
ensembles, as noted.- aRecorded 1956-1964 at Capitol Studios and Radio Recorders,
Hollywood and Fine Recording, New York.- aCompact discs.- aProgram notes by
James Gavin in container.-00gdisc 1.tNight and dayr(Buddy Bregman and orchestra)
--tI get a kick out of your(Paul Smith, piano ; Barney Kessel, guitar ; Joe Mondragon,
bass ; Alvin Stoller, drums) --tBegin the beguine ;tLove for sale ;tMy funny Valentine
;tLady is a tramp ;tWhere or whenr(Buddy Bregman and orchestra) --tTake the
"A" Train ;tI got it bad (and that ain't good)r(Duke Ellington and his orchestra) --tIt
don't mean a thing (if it ain't got that swing)r(Ben Webster, tenor saxophone ; Stuff
Smith, violin ; Paul Smith, piano ; Barney Kessel, guitar ; Joe Mondragon, bass ; Alvin
Stoller, drums) --tCheek to cheekr(Paul Weston and his orchestra).-80gdisc 2.tBlue
skiesr(Paul Weston and his orchestra) --t'S wonderful ;tEmbraceable you ;tI got
rhythm ;tMan I lover(Nelson Riddle and orchestra) --tBlues in the night (My mama
done tol' me) ;tOver the rainbow ;tThat old black magicr(Billy May and orchestra)
--tAll the things you are ;tSkylark ;tToo marvelous for wordsr(Nelson Riddle
and orchestra).- aCompact discs.- 0aJazz.- 0aJazz vocals.- 0aPopular music.-1
aBregman, Buddy.4cnd-1 -aSmith, Paul,d1922-4prf-1 aKessel, Barney.4prf-1
aMondragon, Joe.4prf-1 aStoller, Alvin.4prf-1 -aEllington, Duke,d1899-1974.4prf-1
aWebster, Ben,d1909-1973.4prf-1 aSmith, Stuff.4prf-1 aWeston, Paul,d1912-
1996.4cnd-1 aRiddle, Nelson.4prf-1 aMay, Billy.4prf-2 aBuddy Bregman
Orchestra.4prf-2 -aDuke Ellington Orchestra.4prf-2 aPaul Weston Orchestra.4prf-2
aNelson Riddle Orchestra.4prf-2 aBilly May Orchestra.4prf- aC0bIRU-

FIGURE D.1
Example of raw MARC

Type	a	Elvl	I		Srce		Audn		Ctrl		Lang	por
BLvl	m	Form			Conf	0	Biog		Mrec		Ctry	bl
		Cont	b		Gpub		LitF	0	Indx	1		
Desc	i	Ills	a	b	Fest	0	DtSt	s	Dates	2014		

FIGURE D.2
Example of MARC fixed fields

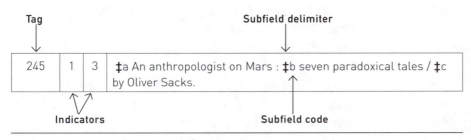

FIGURE D.3
Parts of a MARC variable field

MARC Bibliographic Fields

MARC Bibliographic variable fields are set up so certain tag numbers "rhyme" with each other. Personal names are given in 100, 600, and 700 fields, while corporate body names appear in 110, 610, and 710 fields. Meeting (conference) names are given in 111, 611, and 711 fields, and certain titles appear in 130, 630, 730, and 830 fields. The same rhyming system is used in MARC Authority records, as discussed in chapter 7.

There are hundreds of different MARC Bibliographic fields; which fields are used in a given record depends on the resource the record describes. For example, the record for a DVD will include special MARC fields for the running time of the video, whether it is in color or black and white, its cast members, and so on, while a book has special fields for recording the presence of a bibliography, illustrations, and an index. There are, however, some common MARC fields that are present in many bibliographic records. Here they are, with the most commonly seen codes for each:

Fixed Fields

Type of record: The content of the resource the record describes.

a	Language material (books, magazines)
g	Projected medium (DVDs)
o	Kit
e	Cartographic material (maps, globes)
c	Notated music (sheet music, scores)
i	Non-music sound recording (sound effects CD)
j	Musical sound recording

Bibliographic level: The resource's mode of issuance.

i	Integrating resource
m	Monograph
s	Serial

Descriptive cataloging form: The content standard used when creating the record.

a	AACR2
i	RDA

Encoding level: The degree of completeness of the record blank.

blank	Full-level, input by a Program for Cooperative Cataloging library.
I	Full-level, input by an OCLC participant (OCLC records only)
K	Less-than-full level, input by an OCLC participant (OCLC records only)
M	Less-than-full level, added through a batch process (OCLC records only)
7	Minimal level

Source of cataloging: The type of library that contributed the original record.

blank	Input by a national bibliographic agency (for example, the Library of Congress)
c	Input by a participant in a cooperative cataloging program
d	Other

Language: The language of the resource.

Codes are taken from MARC Code List for Languages
(www.loc.gov/marc/languages/langhome.html).

Place of publication:

Codes are chosen from MARC Code List for Countries
(www.loc.gov/marc/countries).

Type of date/Publication status: In most records, a code that indicates the
kind of dates input in the Date 1 and Date 2 fields; in serials and integrating resources records, the code indicates its publication status.

    s   Single date of publication
            Date 1: publication date
            Date 2: blank

    m   Multiple dates (when a resource is published over more
         than one year)
            Date 1: beginning publication date
            Date 2: ending publication date

    r   Reprint issue date/original date
            Date 1: publication date of reprint
            Date 2: publication date of original

    t   Publication date and copyright date
            Date 1: publication date
            Date 2: copyright date

    c   (for serials and integrating resources only) Resource is cur-
         rently published
            Date 1: date resource began publication
            Date 2: coded '999'

    d   (for serials and integrating resources only) Resource has
         ceased publication
            Date 1: date resource began publication
            Date 2: date resource ceased publication

Date 1: See Type of date/publication status (above).

Date 2: See Type of date/publication status (above).

Variable Fields

020: International Standard Book Number (ISBN)

> Generally used for books, but some other kinds of resources can have ISBNs

022: International Standard Serial Number (ISSN)

> For serials only

024: Other standard identifier

> A place to input Uniform Product Codes (UPC), International Standard Music Numbers, and other standard numbers

040: Source of cataloging

> $a The MARC code for the organization that created the original record (a list of MARC codes for organizations can be found at www.loc.gov/marc/organizations)
>
> $b The language of cataloging—the language used by the cataloger who created the record (not necessarily the same language code as the Language fixed field)
>
> $e Descriptive convention—the content standard used to create the record
>> a—AACR2
>> i—RDA

050: Library of Congress call number (for LCC libraries only)

082: Dewey Decimal Classification number (for DDC libraries only)

090: Library of Congress type call number, not assigned by the Library of Congress (LCC libraries only)

100: Name of author (when author is a person)

110: Name of author (when author is an organization)

111: Name of author (when author is a conference or meeting)

245: Title and statement of responsibility

> **Indicator 1:** Title added entry
>
>> 0   No added entry—This value is used when there is no 1XX field (author field) in the record.

1   Added entry—This value is used when there is a
      1XX field.

Indicator 2: Nonfiling characters

The value in this space tells the ILS how many characters/
spaces to ignore when searching by title. This is important
for titles that begin with articles (i.e., "the," "a," and "an"),
because if those words were not ignored in searching, the
number of records retrieved (just think of how many titles
start with "the") would be overwhelming and not very
useful. The number input in the second indicator space is
the total of the number of characters in the article, plus the
space after the article. This is so the ILS will think the title
starts with the first word after the article.

For example, the title *The Milagro Beanfield War* begins
with "The," an article that has three letters. To determine
the second indicator number, add three plus the one space
following "The" to get four. Now the ILS will ignore the
first four characters or spaces when it searches for this title,
and will think the title is *Milagro Beanfield War.* If five
was accidentally made the second indicator, the ILS would
think the title was *Ilagro Beanfield War.* A library patron
searching for *Milagro Beanfield War* wouldn't retrieve this
record because of the missing letter.

If the title does not start with an article, the second indicator is 0.

$a   First part of title
$b   Remainder of title
$c   Name of author as it appears on the item
$h   General Material Designation (GMD)

         This subfield is used only in AACR2 records for certain
         materials. The most commonly used GMDs are:
             [electronic resource]
             [microform]
             [videorecording]
             [kit]

246: Varying form of title. Sometimes a patron may not find a resource because of the way the title is formatted. For example, the book *The Absence of Colour* has the British English spelling of the word "color" in its title. A cataloger in an American library would be smart to add a 246 field with the American spelling of the title, *Absence of Color*, because a user of his library might not remember to use the English spelling when searching the catalog.

250: Edition statement

260: Publication information (mostly used in AACR2 cataloging)

    $a Place of publication
    $b Publisher
    $c Date of publication

264: Production, Publication, Distribution, Manufacture, and Copyright (mostly used in RDA cataloging)

    $a Place of production, publication, distribution, manufacture
    $b Name of producer, publisher, distributor, manufacturer
    $c Date of production, publication, distribution, manufacture, or copyright

300: Physical description

    $a Extent of the resource

        What is recorded in this subfield differs, depending on the kind of material being described. For example, for a book, the number of pages would go here; for a sound recording, the length of the recording in minutes would go here.

    $b Other physical details

        Like subfield a, what is recorded here differs, depending on the material being described. For example, for a DVD, this is the place to record whether it is in color or black and white, and whether it has sound or is silent. For a book, this is where illustrations are recorded.

    $c Dimensions

        The size of the item. For a book, the height of the spine is given here; for a CD, the diameter of the disc is given; for a map, its height and width are given.

The following three MARC fields are used in RDA records in place of the GMD (MARC 245 $h) used in AACR2 records:

336: Content type (RDA records only)

The type of content of the resource is recorded here. For a book, the content is *text;* for a map it is *cartographic image*; for a music CD it is *performed music.* The terms are chosen from *Term and Code List for RDA Content Types* (www.loc.gov/standards/valuelist/rdacontent.html).

337: Media type (RDA records only)

The medium of the resource (the kind of device, if any, needed to access the resource's content) is recorded here. For a book, the media type is *unmediated*, meaning no device is needed to access its content. For a sound recording, the media type is *audio*, meaning an audio playback device is required to access the content. Terms are chosen from *Term and Code List for RDA Media Types* (www.loc.gov/standards/valuelist/rdamedia.html).

338: Carrier type (RDA records only)

The "container" of the resource's content is recorded here. For a book, the carrier is *volume*, because the text that makes up the book is stored in a physical volume. For a DVD, the carrier is *videodisc*; for a map, the carrier is *sheet.* Terms are chosen from *Term and Code List for RDA Carrier Types* (www.loc.gov/standards/valuelist/rdacarrier.html).

490: Series statement

The series title as found on the resource is transcribed here. The preferred form of the series title may also be recorded in an 830 field.

500: General note

A record may include many different kinds of notes. Among those recorded in the 500 field are:

Where the title in the 245 field was found on the resource
Presence of an index

504: Bibliography note

505: Contents note

508: Production credits (for audiovisual materials)

511: Participant/Performer note (for audiovisual materials)

520: Summary, etc. A note that describes the contents of the resource.

600: Personal name as subject. Used when a person is a subject of a resource.

610: Organization name as subject. Used when an organization is a subject of a resource.

611: Conference/meeting name as subject. Used when a conference or meeting is the subject of a resource.

650: Topical subject term. The term for a topical subject, chosen from a set of preferred subject terms.

651: Geographical subject term. A term for a geographical subject, chosen from a set of preferred subject terms.

700: Personal name. Usually contains names of additional authors, besides the author recorded in field 100.

710: Organization name. Usually contains names of organizations that have an authorship or sponsorship role in the creation of the resource.

711: Conference/meeting name. Usually used when a conference or meeting has some role in the creation of the resource.

776: Additional physical form. This field gives information about different physical forms of the same resource. It is used most often in e-book records to give information about the print version of the book.

780 and 785: Preceding and succeeding entry (serials cataloging only). Serials can change over time, sometimes so significantly that a new catalog record is needed. The most common change is when a serial begins publication under a new title. For example, let's say the magazine *Happy Trails* has been published for several years when the publisher decides to change the name to *Go West*. Under the rules for cataloging serials, this change means *Go West* must have its own, new catalog record. 780 and 785 fields provide links between earlier and later records for the same serial.

780: Preceding (earlier) entry. In the example above, the record for *Go West*, the later title of the serial, would have a 780 field with information about *Happy Trails*, the preceding title.

785: Succeeding (later) entry. The record for *Happy Trails*, the earlier title of the serial, would have a 785 field for *Go West*, because *Go West* succeeded *Happy Trails.*

830: Series added entry, uniform title

You may recall that the 490 field is where a series title is recorded exactly as it appears on the resource. If the series title is "traced," that is, if an access point is needed for it, the series title is entered again in an 830 field. The title in the 830 field is in the form that catalogers have agreed to use for that series, and may be different from what is recorded in the 490 field. For example, the book *Vegan 101: Master Vegan Cooking with 101 Great Recipes* is part of the 101 Series published by Surrey Books. The series title on the book is *Surrey's 101 Series*, so that is what is recorded in the 490 field. However, the agreed-upon form of the series title is *101 series (Surrey Books)*, and the series is traced, so the preferred form is recorded in the 830 field.

856: Electronic location and access. This is where the Uniform Resource Locator (URL) for an online electronic resource, or other online information about a resource (a table of contents, for instance), is recorded.

Indicator 1: Access method. The method of accessing the online information.

4   HTTP—The resource is accessed using Hypertext Transfer Protocol, meaning it is accessed through a web browser.

Indicator 2: Relationship. The relationship of the link to the resource described in the bibliographic record.

0   Resource—The link goes to the resource itself.

1   Version of resource—The link goes to a different version of the resource described in the record,

for example, an electronic version of a print book. Current practice is to use the 776 field for this information.

2   Related resource—The link goes to a resource that is related to the resource represented by the record. For example, the link may go to the electronic form of the table of contents.

$u   Uniform Resource Locator (URL)—The web address of the resource or related resource.

$y   Link text—The text in this subfield replaces the URL in the online catalog. It works like a hypertext link in the catalog.

$z   Public note—A note that is visible in the OPAC.

Here is an example of an 856 field as it appears on the back side of the catalog:

856 | 4 0 | $u http://memory.loc.gov/ammem/wghtml/ wghome.html $y Click here for access. $z Access is not restricted to campus users.

And here is how the same 856 field appears in the public catalog:

Click here for access. Access is not restricted to campus users.

There are many other MARC Bibliographic fields besides those listed above. If you ever have a question about a MARC Bibliographic field, there are helpful guides available online for free (see the list of resources at the end of this appendix).

MARC Holdings

The MARC Holdings format has fewer possible fields than MARC Bibliographic, and the fields do not vary as much by the type of resource. Fixed fields are usually filled in automatically by the ILS, based on information from the bibliographic record and the acquisitions module. For serial records, some variable fields are filled automatically when issues are checked in through the acquisitions module of the ILS, as discussed in chapter 4. Other variable fields are filled in by catalogers. The most common MARC Holdings variable fields are:

852: Location. The resource's location in the library. Its call number and copy number are recorded here.

> **Indicator 1:** Shelving scheme. The classification scheme used to create the call number.
>
> 0   Library of Congress Classification
>
> 1   Dewey Decimal Classification
>
> 3   Superintendent of Documents Classification (for US government documents)
>
> **Indicator 2:** Shelving order. Defines whether a serial or multi-part item has more than one numbering scheme.
>
> blank   No information provided
>
> 0   Not enumeration
>
> 1   Primary enumeration—The item has only one numbering scheme (this code is used for most resources).
>
> 2   Alternative enumeration—The item has two numbering schemes and is shelved by the secondary scheme.
>
> **$a**   Location. The institution holding the resource. Many libraries do not code this field, because everything in a library's catalog is understood to be at the same at the same institution.
>
> **$b**   Sublocation or collection. The specific location within the library where the resource is shelved. This is usually one of a set of locally devised codes. Examples of sublocations are: Children's Room, Reference Area, and General Stacks.
>
> **$h**   Classification part. The first part of the call number.
>
> **$i**   Item part. The remaining part of the call number, usually the final Cutter number and the date of publication.
>
> **$t**   Copy number. Which copy of the resource is represented by the holdings record. Not all libraries use copy numbers.
>
> **$x**   Nonpublic note. A note about the copy represented by the holdings record that does not display in the online catalog.

$z Public note. A note about the copy represented by the holdings record that does display in the online catalog.

To illustrate, an 852 field for the book *The Man Who Mistook His Wife for a Hat* might look something like this:

852 | 0 1 | $b General stacks $h RC351 $i .S195 1998 $t Copy 2 $x Cover is torn.

853/863: Captions and Pattern/Enumeration and Chronology—Basic bibliographic unit (mostly used for serials holdings)

The 853 and 863 fields give holdings information in finely parsed way, that is, with only small units of information in each subfield. The 853 field contains "captions," or labels, for the parts of a serial or multipart monograph that are held by the library. Captions are almost abbreviated, for example, "v." for volume, and "no." for number. There are often multiple 863 fields for one 853 field. The 863 field contains the "enumeration" that goes with the captions—the numbers of the volumes, numbers, etc., held by the library, as well as the "chronology," the dates associated with the items held by the library. The information in these two fields display together in the OPAC. For example, the journal *Cataloging and Classification Quarterly* is issued in volumes and numbers. If a library holds Volume 21, Number 2 (1996) through Volume 51, no. 8 (2014), but Volume 32, number 2 (2001) is missing, the 853 and 863 fields would look like this on the back side of the catalog:

853     $a v. $b no. $i (year)
863     $a 21-32 $b 2-1$i 1996-2000
863     $a 33-51 $b 1-8 $i 2002-2014

On the front side of the catalog, the three fields would combine to display like this:

v.21, no.2-v.23, no.1 (1996-2000)
v.33, no.1-v.51, no.8 (2001-2014)

866: Textual Holdings—Basic bibliographic unit

Holdings information may be also given in a non-parsed-out way. When that is the case, fields 866, 867, and 868 are used.

The information in these fields in the OPAC displays in a way similar to the 853/863 fields. Using 866 fields to record the holdings for *Cataloging and Classification Quarterly* from the example above, the 866 fields would look like this on the back side of the catalog:

```
866     $a v.21:no.2(1996)-v.23:no.1(2000),
866     $a v.33:no.1(2000)-v.51:no.8(2014)
```

Copy holdings records are always either linked to a bibliographic record or embedded in it, depending on the ILS. If you have questions about MARC Holdings records, the MARC 21 Format for Holdings Data website (www.loc .gov/marc/holdings) has detailed information about each field and subfield.

RESOURCES

Bibliographic Formats and Standards. 4th ed., revised. Dublin, OH: OCLC, 2008. www.oclc.org/bibformats/en.html.
"Understanding MARC Bibliographic: Machine-Readable Cataloging." 8th ed. Washington: DC: Library of Congress, 2009. www.loc.gov/marc/umb.
MARC 21 Format for Bibliographic Data. www.loc.gov/marc/bibliographic.
MARC 21 Format for Holdings Data. www.loc.gov/marc/holdings.

Glossary

AACR, AACR2, AACR2R. *See Anglo-American Cataloguing Rules.*

Abstract. A brief summary of the content of a resource.

Access point. A searchable unit of information in a catalog record.

Acquisitions. The unit in many technical services departments that coordinates ordering and receipt of new materials. It may also be either a stand-alone department or part of the collection development department.

Aggregator. A company that takes content from several producers and aggregates, or combines it onto one platform. An aggregator also adds value by providing indexing and abstracting services.

Allocation. The part of a budget that is reserved for a particular area.

Analysis. The process of cataloging the parts of a resource separately, with each part having its own record.

Anglo-American Cataloguing Rules (AACR) and its revisions (AACR2, AACR2R). A cataloging content standard first published in 1967, with revisions issued through 2002. The *Anglo-American Cataloguing Rules* were widely adopted in the United States, Canada, the United Kingdom, and Australia.

Attribute. In *Functional Requirements for Bibliographic Records* (FRBR) and *Resource Description and Access* (RDA), a characteristic of an entity or relationship.

Audiovisual (AV). A shorthand term for all formats that are not either traditional or electronic books or serials. These formats include audiobooks, DVDs, music CDs, Blu-ray discs, software, and video games.

Authority control. The practice of establishing one unique form for a name, title, or subject term, and using that form consistently in library catalogs.

Authority file. A database made up of individual authority records.

Authority record. A MARC record that records the preferred form of a name, title, or subject term, and includes variant forms ("See" and "See also" references) and citations for the sources used to make the decision about the preferred form.

Available. A status many vendors use to indicate materials they have on hand for immediate shipment.

Backorder. A status many vendors use to indicate materials they do not have on hand, but have contacted their suppliers to get additional copies.

Bar code. A label with variously patterned bars that is machine readable. In libraries, bar codes serve as a unique identifier of the item to which they are attached.

Bibliographic Framework Initiative (BIBFRAME). An initiative to replace Machine-Readable Cataloging (MARC) with a new data format for bibliographic information that relies on linked data.

Bibliographic record. An entry in a library's catalog that describes and provides access to a resource.

Bibliographic utility. An organization that maintains a huge database of bibliographic records that are contributed and copied by participating libraries.

Bibliography. A list, in a consistent citation style, of sources consulted.

Budget. A forecast of expected revenues coupled with a plan for how to expend those revenues.

Budget formula. A set criteria for determining how to allocate expected revenues.

Call number. A code, often unique, assigned to a library resource by a cataloger. A call number usually consists of a subject classification code, one or more cutter numbers, and a date.

Carrier. In *Resource Description and Access* (RDA), a resource's physical storage medium.

Catalog. A complete list of the holdings of a library, arranged to help users find library resources.

Cataloging. The process of creating or copying bibliographic records for inclusion in a library's catalog.

Cataloging-in-Publication. A program of the Library of Congress and other libraries in which catalog records are created for resources before they are published.

Centralized list generation. A means of selecting materials for a library in which each selector builds her order from a list developed by a centralized office, usually collection development.

Centralized selection. A means of selecting materials for a library in which all selection is done by a single person or small group of people for the entire library.

Character encoding standard. In computing, a group of symbols used to display text electronically.

Claiming. The process of reporting that an issue of a serial was not received.

Classification. The process of dividing the world of knowledge into hierarchical classes and subclasses; also refers to assigning a classification number to a resource.

Classification system. A system of numeric or alphanumeric codes for arranging library materials by subject.

Collection development. The process by which materials are selected for a library collection. Often this term is used interchangeably with collection management.

Collection management. The set of processes by which a library adds and removes materials from their collection.

Collection turnover. How often a collection circulates during a set period of time. If a collection has 2,000 items and circulation of 10,000, the collection turnover would be 5.

Collocation. The process of bringing together resources that have the same author, subject, classification, or series title.

Conference name. *See* Meeting name.

Consortium. A group of libraries that join together to work towards a single, shared goal.

Content standard. A set of guidelines for describing resources and creating access points.

Content type. In *Resource Description and Access* (RDA), the fundamental form of communication in which the content of a resource is expressed, and the human sense through which it is perceived.

Controlled vocabulary. A list of preferred terms used in catalog records. Controlled vocabularies may consist of subject terms, such as the *Sears List of Subject Headings*, or other kinds of terms, such as the lists of terms used for content, medium, and carrier in RDA.

Cooperative cataloging. *See* Shared cataloging.

Copy cataloging. Copying (and perhaps editing) a bibliographic record that already exists.

Copy holdings record. A record linked to a bibliographic record that contains information about where a resource is located, its call number, its copy number, and (for multipart resources) what parts the library owns.

Copyright date. The year in which a work was first published, usually indicated by the symbol © or the letter c, followed by the year.

Corporate body. An organization that has a name and acts as one entity.

Cross-reference. A reference from one heading to another.

Cutter number. A code made up of letter(s) and numbers that is added to a call number to help maintain alphabetical order. Sometimes called a "Cutter."

Deaccession. *See* Deselection.

Decentralized selection. A method of selecting materials in a library that allows each selector to work independently, with no collection development office overseeing their activities.

Degreed librarian. A librarian who has received a master's degree in librarianship. This could be a Master of Library Science (MLS), Master of Library and Information Science (MLIS), Master of Science in Librarianship (MSL), or a number of other iterations.

Delimiter. In Machine-Readable Cataloging (MARC), a symbol that marks the beginning of a subfield.

Descriptive cataloging. The part of cataloging in which information about a resource is recorded in sufficient detail that a user can distinguish it from a similar resource and determine if it is the resource he wants. Descriptive cataloging includes the creation of non-subject access points. *See also* Subject cataloging.

Deselection. The process of removing materials from the library collection. Also called weeding or deaccession,

Dewey Decimal Classification. A library classification system devised by Melvil Dewey comprising ten main subject classes, each of which represents a broad area of knowledge. Each class is made up of ten subclasses that represent narrower areas of knowledge. In turn, each subclass has ten sub-subclasses, each of which represents an even narrower area of knowledge.

Disambiguation. In authority work, the process of differentiating similar names, titles, or subject terms from one another.

Discount. The price decrease vendors give their customers as a reward for doing business with them.

Discovery service. A way of searching all the resources a library owns or has access to through a single interface.

Distributed selection. A means of selecting materials for a library in which all selection is done by a group of people working independently.

E-book. A textual monograph in electronic form.

EDI. *See* Electronic Data Interface.

Edition. All copies of a resource that have the exact same content, format, and publisher.

Electronic Data Interface. A protocol for sharing information between different computer systems.

Electronic Resources Management System (ERMS). A system, usually a database, designed to allow for the efficient management of a library's electronic resources, such as databases, electronic serials, e-books, downloadable books, streaming music, streaming video, etc.

Encoding level. The level of completeness of a Machine-Readable Cataloging (MARC) record.

Encumbrance. Money that is reserved for orders already placed. If the orders are canceled or are received with a price lower than the encumbrance, the money is returned to the available budget.

Endpapers. The papers that form the hinges connecting the textblock to the cover of a hardback book.

Entity. In *Functional Requirements for Bibliographic Records* (FRBR) and *Resource Description and Access* (RDA), something that exists as a discrete unit. Bibliographic entities include persons, subjects, and works.

ERMS. *See* Electronic Resources Management System.

Export. To electronically copy a record, usually from a bibliographic utility to a local catalog.

Extent. In cataloging, the number and kind of units that make up a resource.

Field. In Machine-Readable Cataloging (MARC), a unit of bibliographic description that contains a defined type of information about a resource. A MARC field may be "fixed"—of a predetermined length, or "variable"—with no predetermined length.

Fill rate. The percentage of the orders placed with a vendor that are actually filled.

Fixed field. In a Machine-Readable Cataloging (MARC) record, a field of fixed length.

Flyleaves. The parts of a dust jacket that are folded into a book to hold the dust jacket on. In the United States, flyleaves usually include a statement about the book and a brief biography of the author.

Formula-based budgeting. A method of budget allocation that assigns various weights to different factors, and then plugs those weights and factors into a formula.

FRBR. *See Functional Requirements for Bibliographic Records.*

Front matter. Information that appears prior to the beginning of the text of an item. It usually includes the title page, acknowledgments, foreword, and so forth.

***Functional Requirements for Bibliographic Records* (FRBR).** A conceptual model of the bibliographic universe, based on the entity-relationship model from database science. FRBR is one of the bases of *Resource Description and Access* (RDA).

Funding agency. The fiscal entity that provides the money used to run a library.

General material designation (GMD). Under the *Anglo-American Cataloguing Rules*, a term given in the Title and Statement of Responsibility area that indicates the broad class of materials to which a resource belongs. GMDs are added only for certain kinds of materials, for example, electronic resources, microforms, and video recordings.

GMD. *See* General Material Designation.

Gutter. The channel formed by the combined margin space of the facing pages of an item.

Heading. A type of access point. A heading may be a personal name, a corporate body name, a title, or a subject term.

Hinge. The connection between the front and back covers of a hardback book and the text block.

Holdings record. *See* Copy holdings record.

ILS. *See* Integrated Library System.

Import. In cataloging, to electronically bring a record into a local catalog, usually from a bibliographic utility.

Indicator. In Machine-Readable Cataloging (MARC) variable fields, one of two characters that follow the MARC tag; the meaning of an indicator depends on the MARC field it is part of.

Integrated Library System. An integrated set of computer applications that perform the behind-the-scenes work of a library. An Integrated Library System usually includes software for acquisitions, cataloging, circulation, and a public catalog.

Integrating resource. A resource in which new content is integrated into the whole, leaving the resource somewhat changed but essentially the same.

International Standard Book Number (ISBN). A unique ten- or thirteen-digit number created in compliance with international standards and assigned to a single edition of a monographic resource.

International Standard Serial Number (ISSN). A unique eight-digit number created in compliance with international standards and assigned to a serial resource.

Internet Protocol (IP) address. The unique address of a particular computer.

Invoice. Documentation from a vendor of how much it is charging for an item and how much the library owes for it.

ISBN. *See* International Standard Book Number.

ISSN. *See* International Standard Serial Number.

Item record. A record linked to a copy holdings record that represents one unit (for example, one volume) of a resource. An item record may include a bar code, a copy number, item type, and location.

Journal. A kind of serial. A journal is a multipart subscription publication that usually has a research or academic focus.

Keyword, key word. A significant word or phrase in a bibliographic record that may be used when searching a library's catalog.

Library Management System. *See* Integrated Library System, Library Services Platform.

Library of Congress Classification. An alphanumeric classification system developed at the Library of Congress that divides the world of knowledge into twenty classes, each of which breaks down that area of knowledge into smaller and smaller divisions.

***Library of Congress Subject Headings* (LCSH).** A list of general use subject terms used at the Library of Congress and many other libraries in the United States. The *Library of Congress Subject Headings* includes "See" and "See also" references that direct users from variant forms of a term to the preferred form of the term, and to related subject terms.

Library Services Platform. A "next generation" Integrated Library System that integrates a discovery service and electronic resources management.

Library user. *See* Patron.

License. A legal document defining the rights and responsibilities of both parties regarding the usage of different types of products.

Linked data. Data that is structured and linked together in such a way that it may be "understood" by computers.

Local practices. The collection of standard and nonstandard practices at a particular library. Local practices may be used in cataloging, acquisitions, circulation, and other areas of the library.

Machine-Readable Cataloging (MARC). A standard digital format that gives catalog information a structure, allows it to be exchanged between libraries, and enables it to be displayed in an online catalog.

MARC, MARC 21. *See* Machine-Readable Cataloging.

MARC-8. A character set used in Machine-Readable Cataloging (MARC).

Match point. A key piece of information that should be identical on a resource and in the bibliographic record that describes the resource.

Materials budget. The part of the library budget that is devoted to the purchase and subscription to items housed in or accessed through the library.

Media type. In *Resource Description and Access* (RDA), a category that reflects the general type of device required to access the content of a resource.

Meeting name. The name given to a formal meeting of people. Also called a conference name. Because meetings often recur, the name of a meeting may be qualified by a date, a location, or both.

Metadata. Structured information that describes a resource or resources. Although catalog information is a kind of metadata, in libraries this term is used to refer to non-cataloging metadata.

Mode of issuance. The way in which a resource is published. A resource may be published as a monograph, as a serial, as an integrating resource, or as part of a series.

Module. A part of an Integrated Library System devoted to a single functional area.

Monograph. A resource that is complete in itself, either in one part or a defined number of parts.

Mylar. A type of plastic film used to protect and reinforce the covers and bindings of library materials.

Note. In cataloging, a statement, usually given in a 5XX field in a bibliographic record, to provide more information about the resource, or explain something in another part of the bibliographic record.

OCLC. The world's largest bibliographic utility. Founded in 1967 as the Online Computer Library Center, OCLC is a non-profit membership organization.

Online Public Access Catalog (OPAC). The side of a library's catalog that is visible to, and searchable by the public.

OOP. *See* Out of print.

OOS. *See* Out of stock.

OPAC. *See* Online Public Access Catalog.

Open access. A current trend in publishing that allows for unrestricted access and unrestricted reuse of various types of materials.

Order confirmation. A message from a vendor stating that an order has been received, which usually includes some indication of publication status.

Ordering. The process of notifying a vendor that you wish to purchase or subscribe to a particular item.

Original cataloging. In cataloging, creating a new record from scratch, as opposed to copy cataloging (copying an existing record).

Out of print (OOP). A publication status indicating that an item is no longer being produced by the publisher/producer.

Out of stock (OOS). A publication status indicating that an item is not currently in stock at a vendor's warehouse, but that it is still available.

Outsourcing. Contracting with a vendor to provide a service to a library. Authority control and cataloging are the most commonly outsourced technical services activities.

Packing slip. A list of all the materials in a single shipment from a vendor.

Paraprofessionals. Staff in positions that require a higher level of knowledge and experience than unskilled clerk positions.

Patron. One of many terms used for a library user. Other terms include customer, end user, or user.

PCC. *See* Program for Cooperative Cataloging.

Periodical. A kind of serial. A periodical is a multipart subscription received on an ongoing basis.

Physical processing. The part of preparing materials for circulation that involves the addition of labels, stamps, jackets, and any other additions that require physically handling the item.

Policy. A document that defines the choices an organization has made from a variety of possible choices.

Preceding title. In the successive entry method of cataloging serials, the previous record in the sequence of records for a serial.

Preferred form. The word or phrase selected to be used consistently to represent a specific name, title, or subject in library catalogs.

Prepublication. In cataloging, an encoding level indicating that the bibliographic record was created before the resource it describes was published.

Procedure. A document that defines the accepted methods of operation of an organization.

Professional librarian. *See* Degreed librarian.

Program for Cooperative Cataloging (PCC). An international organization of libraries that work together to create original catalog records for newly published materials in a timely manner.

Property stamp. Usually rubber stamps embossed with the name of the library that owns an item. This term may also mean the actual stamp left behind on the object by a property stamp.

Proxy server. A computer server that acts as an intermediary between a patron seeking an electronic resource and the resource itself. The purpose is to limit the use of certain licensed electronic resources to patrons who have borrowing privileges. Each patron is authenticated by logging in with identifying information and a password.

Publication status. Information provided by the publisher or vendor to inform you if the title you ordered is available.

Purchase order. A document from a funding agency authorizing an organization to order materials from a vendor.

Qualifier. In authority work, information added to a name, title, or subject term to differentiate it from similar names, titles, or subject terms. Qualifiers are given in parentheses.

Queries. A way of programming report writing modules in many ILSs.

Radio frequency identification (RFID). A method of tagging materials that combines the security target and the bar code with one tag.

RDA. *See Resource Description and Access.*

Record structure. In a library catalog, the hierarchical relationship between bibliographic, copy holdings, and (if present) item records.

Resource. Any item collected by a library.

Resource Description and Access (RDA). A content standard published in 2010 that incorporates the principles of *Functional Requirements for Bibliographic Records.*

RFID. *See* radio frequency identification.

Sears List of Subject Headings. A list of general subject terms based on the *Library of Congress Subject Headings.*

Security tag. A target attached to a library resource so it will be detectable by the security system installed in the library.

"See also" reference. A cross-reference that refers users from one preferred form of a name, title, or subject to a related preferred form of a name, title, or subject.

"See" reference. A cross-reference that refers users from a variant form of a name, title, or subject term to the preferred form of that name, title, or subject.

Selection. The process used of choosing which materials should be ordered for the library.

Semi-centralized selection. A hybrid selection methodology that combines centralized list generation with decentralized selection.

Serial. A resource issued in discrete parts over time, with no predetermined end, and usually bearing numbers, dates, or both.

Series. A group of related materials, each with its own individual title as well as a series title, published by the same publisher, and often bearing a series number.

Series title. The title of a series. Series titles often have a preferred form.

Shared cataloging. Also called cooperative cataloging. The practice of sharing catalog records between libraries, made possible by shared cataloging standards and bibliographic utilities.

Shelflisting. In cataloging, adjusting the Cutter number of a resource to place its call number in alphabetic order on the shelf or in the catalog list of call numbers.

Signature. A stack of paper that is printed with multiple pages and then folded and cut so that the pages are in order. The text block of a hardback book is usually made up of multiple signatures.

SkyRiver. A bibliographic utility founded in 2009.

Spine. The narrow part of the binding that is joined to the book.

Spine label. The label attached to the spine of the item. Usually this includes the call number.

Standard. A set of agreed-upon practices, spelled out in detail in textual documentation.

Standard digital format. An agreed-upon digital framework that gives catalog records a structure and allows them to be displayed and transmitted by computers. Machine-Readable Cataloging (MARC) is a standard digital format.

Statement of responsibility. In descriptive cataloging, the area of a record that gives the name or names of the person, persons, or corporate body responsible for creating a resource.

Subfield. In Machine-Readable Cataloging (MARC), a subdivision of a variable field; each subfield begins with a delimiter and has an alphabetical or numeric code.

Subheading. A division added to a subject term to make it more specific.

Subject cataloging. The part of cataloging in which subject access to a resource is provided by assigning a classification number and subject terms to the record that represents the resource. *See also* Descriptive cataloging.

Subject heading. An access point in a bibliographic record that consists of the preferred term for a subject. May include subdivisions to make the heading more specific.

Succeeding title. In the successive entry method of cataloging serials, the next following record in a sequence of records for a serial.

Successive entry. A method of cataloging serials in which a new title is created whenever the serial undergoes a major change such as a significant change of title or change of issuing body. The result is a sequence of bibliographic records for the same serial. Most US libraries use successive entry for serials cataloging.

Table. A method of data storage used by integrated library systems and other database systems.

Tag. In Machine-Readable Cataloging (MARC), a three-digit numeric code assigned to a variable field to define the kind of information contained in the field.

Target. *See* Security tag.

Technical services. The department in many libraries that is responsible for acquisitions, cataloging, and physical processing. It can also include other areas, such as collection development.

Text block, textblock. The collection of signatures or pages that make up the content of a book. They are bound together and attached to covers, creating a complete book.

Tip/tipping in. A method used to insert replacement pages or reattach loose pages in an item. This process is performed by putting glue on the edges (tips) of a page so it will adhere to other pages in the gutter.

Title page. Part of the front matter of a book, this page consists of full title, author(s), editor(s), translator(s), and other people important to the creation of the content of the book. It may also include publication information.

Topical subject heading. A subject heading for a topic.

Trace. In cataloging, to record the preferred form, or heading, of a piece of information in a bibliographic record.

Tracking. The process by which materials on order are followed through the vendor's and shipper's systems.

Trial subscription. Temporary access to a product for evaluation purposes.

Uniform Resource Locator (URL). An Internet address.

Uniform title. In authority control, the preferred, unique form of a title. A series title is a kind of uniform title.

Universal Product Code. A bar code that appears on most products, and used for a variety of purposes. Universal Product Codes cannot be used for library inventory purposes, because all copies of each edition will have the same code.

UPC. *See* Universal Product Code.

URL. *See* Uniform Resource Locator.

User. *See* Patron.

UTF-8. A character set used in Machine-Readable Cataloging (MARC) that supports Unicode, an international standard for textual characters.

Value-added services (VAS). Services performed by vendors that add value to the products they sell.

Variable field. In Machine-Readable Cataloging (MARC), a field with a three-digit tag, indicators, and subfields. A variable field has no predetermined number of characters.

Vendor. A company that does business with an organization.

Verification. The process used to confirm the information used to order materials.

Weeding. *See* Deselection.

Workflow. The sequence of processes through which a piece of work passes from initiation to completion.

Index

in physical processing, 121–122
in systems, 17
trial subscription, 38, 39, 69–70
typographical errors, 137, 143

U

Ulrich's Periodical Directory, 34, 35, 66
UlrichsWeb, 34
undergraduate students, xi
UN/EDIFACT (United Nations rules for
Electronic Data Interchange for
Administration, Commerce and
Transport), 17
Unicode, 169–170
Uniform Resource Locator (URL)
definition of, 80
fields for electronic resources records,
99, 102
removing/correcting dead links in
catalog, 143
testing 856 field link, 103
uniform title, 124, 127, 131–134
update
of collection development policy, 20
to national authority file, 140–141
of serials check-in record, 69
usage statistics, 16
UTF-8, 170

V

value-added services, 45
variable fields
MARC Bibliographic fields, 172,
175–181
of MARC Holdings, 181–184
of MARC records, 170
parts of MARC variable field, 172
variables, of formula-based budgeting,
53–54
vendors
acquisitions from, 57–59

approval plans, DDA/PDA, 26, 27
authority work outsourcing to, 141–142
care/feeding of, 59
communication with, 6–7
definition of, 45
library materials vendors, 57–58
ordering monographs from, 60–64
outsourced cataloging, 104–105
serials, selection of, 34, 35
serials acquisition process, 64–69
technical services functions offered
by, x
tools for limiting publication universe, 26
verification, in acquisitions, 60–61,
66–67, 70
video recordings, 93–94
See also DVD
Virtual International Authority File (VIAF),
144, 145
vocabulary. *See* terms, specialized

W

weeding. *See* deselection (weeding)
wet materials, 153
withdrawals, 142, 149
workflow
for cataloging electronic materials, 77
for cataloging physical materials, 76
of collection development, 19
definition of, 3
of monograph acquisitions, 60
organization of technical services
departments and, 3
of serials acquisition, 65
of technical services departments, 9–10
workflow chart, 9–10
WorldCat, 35, 61, 66

Z

034 field, 135